中国人在硅谷

—NetScreen的故事

陈怀临

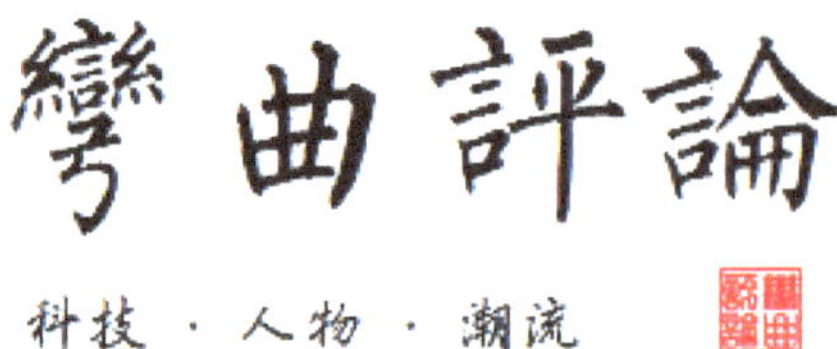

The Chinese in Silicon Valley

Author: Huailin Chen

ISBN: 978-1539774594
10 9 8 7 6 5 4 3 2 1
1. Chinese 2. Silicon Valley 3. Network Security
November, 2016 First Edition
Printed in CreateSpace
Web: www DOT valleytalk DOT org
Email：huailin AT gmail DOT com

谨以此书献给NetScreen Alumni

Old soldiers never die; they just fade away.

—General Douglas MacArthur

老兵不死，只是凋零。

—道格拉斯·麦克阿瑟

目录

我冷眼向过去稍稍回顾,
只见它曲折灌溉的悲喜
都消失在一片亘古的荒漠,
这才知道我的全部努力
不过完成了普通的生活。

一穆旦 。《冥想》

前言

1997年10月，来自中国大陆的三个年轻工程师邓锋(北极光创投创始人和董事总经理)，柯严(北极光创投创始人和投资合伙人)，谢青(美国网络安全公司Fortinet的创始人，CEO和董事长)在美国硅谷共同创建了网屏技术有限公司(NetScreen Technologies Inc)。在之后的6年4个月里，一批以来自中国大陆为主体的华人工程师研发队伍在美国的硅谷演绎了一个从无到有，从弱小到壮大，从在美国NADAQ上市到被Juniper Networks以41亿美金高价并购的传奇故事。

(NetScreen在IPO时的办公大楼，位于硅谷的Sunnyvale)

网屏技术有限公司是一个研发和销售网络安全系统软件和设备的公司。其产品为Firewall/IPSEC VPN，IDP，SSL/VPN等系列。与其他 业界网络安全公司的产品比较，NetScreen采用了硬件加速，基于ASIC芯片的快速通路（Fast Path）与传统CPU担任慢速通路（Slow Path）相结合的系统体系结 构。这种快速通路与慢速通路分离的体系结构，使得NetScreen在商业上获得了巨大的成功，在高端Firewall/VPN市场上，NetScreen的产品稳定在领先地位。在全球网络安全产品市场上，位居第二，仅落后于思科（Cisco）。

（NetScreen曾经位于硅谷高速公路237旁边的办公大楼）

NetScreen切入市场的战略上首先定位在企业的中低端产品线，然后迅速的通过ASIC芯片加速技术进入了高端产品线市场，并极力凸显其产品的性能优势，形成在市场上的竞争力。

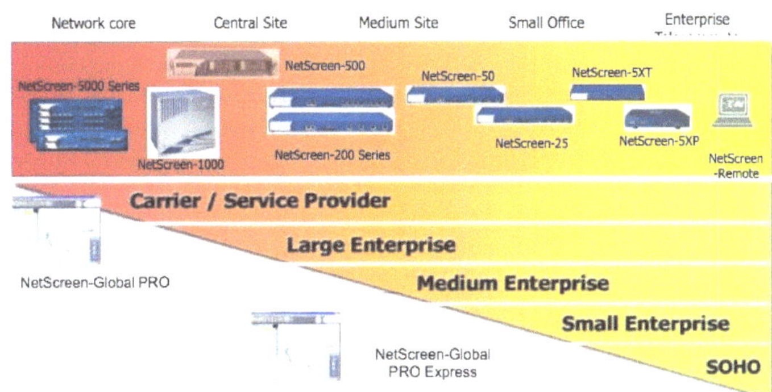

(NetScreen的网络安全产品覆盖企业和运营商的各个领域)

2001年12月12日，NetScreen在NASDAQ上市，其股票代号为NSCN。

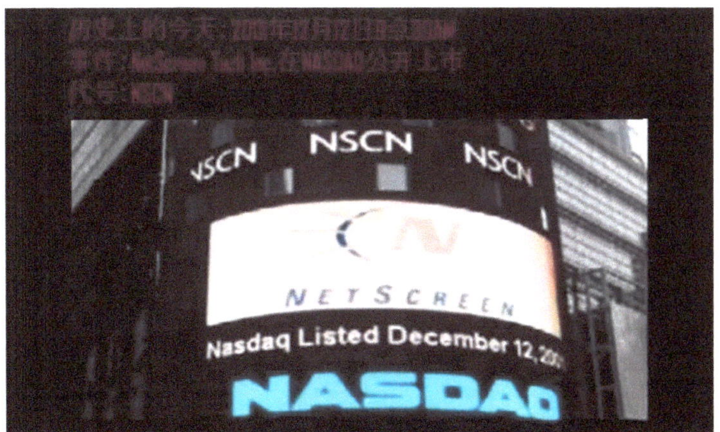

(2001年12月12日，NetScreen上市时NASDAQ交易所)

第一天，股票开盘价位$23.76，收盘价位于$23.14。总交易量达 6 百万股。公司市值为17亿美金。

下面的这张照片是当年NetScreen上市时，在Sunnyvale的员工合影。第一排中间（前排左五）的是邓锋。前排右六是柯严。

(NetScreen上市时在美国总部的全体员工合影)

（创办人邓锋与CEO，VP Sales等高管庆祝上市成功）

（创办人柯严与CFO等高管庆祝上市成功）

（NetScreen员工在庆祝公司上市）

（NetScreen员工在庆祝公司上市）

（NetScreen员工在庆祝公司上市）

（NetScreen员工在庆祝公司上市）

（NetScreen员工在庆祝公司上市）

NetScreen成功上市后，业务迅速发展，不断推出各种高中端防火墙产品，并连续收购了2家初创公司，分别为做IDP的OneSecure和做SSL/VPN的公司Neoteris。截至2003年底，公司营业额高达2.45亿美金，公司已经赢利5千万美金。公司手里有3.7亿的现金。股票在NASDAQ市场上市值24亿美金。

在NetScreen各方面快速发展的2001-2003年，历史出现了重大拐弯。2004年2月9日，全球第二大网络通讯设备公司 Juniper Networks 以NetScreen 股票NSCN 2月6日收盘市值26.40美金为基点，出价约41亿美金并购NetScreen，引起了全球通讯和安全市场的巨大轰动。并购案于当年4月完成。

NetScreen在研发，市场都在最高峰的时候，被Juniper高溢价收购，使得NetScreen的独立发展做大做强，成为一个百亿美金的网络安全公司的机会失去了可能。

如果Juniper并购NetScreen之后，NetScreen产品线能够在一个更大的市场空间得以发展壮大，也不失为一个好的结合。但过去的十年，Juniper的网络安全产品线的发展成为一个令人扼腕的故事，痛失了先发优势和许多良机。

截至2016年，网络安全产品线已经是连续6年的业绩下滑。而以此同时，NetScreen当年的，和后来的竞争对手公司(含从NetScreen分离出来的创业公司)，例如，Checkpoint(以色列公司)，Fortinet(由NetScreen的创办人之一谢青创办)， PaloAlto Networks， FireEye公司等，抓住了发展机遇，迅速培养新市场，并在UTM市场，NGFW， APT市场，推出新概念，打造新的产品，使得网络安全产业蓬勃发展，欣欣向荣。从某种意义上而言，这也是NetScreen的历史贡献之一。牺牲了自己，造就了网络安全界的一个生态链。

Juniper Networks, Inc. to Acquire NetScreen Technologies, Inc.

Combination provides comprehensive, best-in-class networking solutions

Monday February 9, 2004 5:08 am PST

Dateline:

SUNNYVALE, Calif.

Public Company Information:

NASDAQ:JNPR

Juniper Networks, Inc. (Nasdaq: JNPR) has signed an agreement to acquire NetScreen Technologies, Inc. (Nasdaq: NSCN) in a stock-for-stock merger transaction. Based upon Juniper Networks closing stock price of $29.47 on February 6, 2004, the deal has an approximate value of $4 billion. Juniper Networks stock will be exchanged for NetScreen Technologies stock at a fixed exchange ratio of 1.404 shares of Juniper Networks common stock for each outstanding share of NetScreen Technologies common stock. The combined company will provide customers with mission critical networking requirements, including security, reliability and performance, each simultaneously without compromise.

"Our collective customers have told us security, reliability and performance are mission critical to their network users, and together we will deliver a compelling response to their needs."

（Juniper并购NetScreen的新闻稿）

2014年1月，华尔街著名的对冲基金Elliott Management发布了一个很有影响力的调查报告--"Juniper Networks--Elliott Management's Perspectives"。调查报告对Juniper过去10年公司业绩一直低迷做出了详尽的分析，并提出了重要的改革建议。其中，对Juniper收购NetScreen之后的许多错误重组做出了很严肃的批评。调查报告明确指出，如果NetScreen产品线单独发展，一定会比目前更好。

NetScreen被收购10年后，当年的创办人，管理团队，研发和市场许多人员逐渐离开了Juniper，创办了自己的投资基金公司，创业公司或者融入了硅谷的其他高科技公司。在硅谷，在美国网络安全界，NetScreen的同事们互相提携，互相帮助，逐渐发展成为一个“NetScreen圈子”，积极的影响着全世界范围内的网络安全产业。

NetScreen创办人邓锋与柯严在2004年下半年低调离开Juniper，并开始在投资领域发展。北极光创投创办以来，投资了许多著名的公司，例如，展讯，汉庭，美团，中科创达等。伴随着高速发展的中国经济快速成长。目前，旗下管理资产总额近100亿美金。

NetScreen另外一个创办人谢青在1999年离开公司后，创办了网络安全公司Fortinet，聚焦在AV，IPS，Firewall集成在一起的UTM系统。Fortinet于2009年在NASDAQ上市，目前市值为51亿美金。

NetScreen从上市到并购，经历了总共589天。作为一个单独的公司实体已经消失在历史中。但是，NetScreen，一个以来自中国大陆为主体的工程师队伍,共同创建的历史和文化，在持续影响着现在的和将来的华人创业者们。

本书聚焦于NetScreen公司史料的研究与分析，是一本着眼于高科技公司发展的各个阶段，各种维度，来考察一个硅谷公司的研究性书籍。与其他中文励志书籍不同之处在于，本书秉承客观数据，不歌功颂德，也不妄自菲薄，力图呈现NetScreen公司当年的各方面，让读者从作者收集，整理和研究分析的数据中，从历史往事考据中，去领略一段中国人在硅谷的故事。

第一章 团队结构

1997年10月，邓锋(Deng Feng)，柯严(Ke Yan)，谢青(Xie Qing)(作者注：排名按姓氏DKX字母序)共同创建了网屏技术有限公司(NetScreen Technologies Inc)。
1998年10月，投资NetScreen的红杉资本引入Robert Thomas加入NetScreen，并出任CEO & President。其时NetScreen Inc.员工为38人。32人为中国工程师。
强势VC的介入，希望公司能够加快销售和市场的发展。后来NetScreen上市时的高管基本上来自98年之后加入的。
1999年9月，谢青，NetScreen三共同创始人之一，因为各种原因离开了NetScreen。之后，谢青于2000年创办了UTM产品公司Fortinet。
之后的6年零4个月里，由邓锋（出任董事会成员和研发副总裁），柯严（出任公司副总裁和首席架构师）领导下的，以来自中国大陆和台湾为主体的NetScreen研发团队在美国的硅谷共同演绎了一个从无到有，从弱小到壮大，从上市到被高价收购的传奇故事。

高管和董事会

NetScreen上市时，最开始的创办人只剩下了2位（邓锋 柯严）。CEO是1998年10月董事会请来的Robert Thomas。下面列出的是NetScreen公司申请上市时S-1报表中公司管理层团队，总共16人。从某种意义上而言，NetScreen是一个华裔创办，以华裔为研发主体，白人为管理团队为主的硅谷公司。

名字	职务
------	--- --------
Robert D. Thomas..........	President, Chief Executive Officer and Director
Remo E. Canessa............	Chief Financial Officer and Corporate Secretary
Charles R. Clark................	Vice President of Operations
Feng Deng..........................	Vice President of Engineering and Director
David K. Flynn.................	Vice President of Marketing
James K. Gifford.............	Vice President of Systems and Services
Yan Ke..............................	Vice President and Chief Architect
Edie R. Rodriguez.............	Vice President of HR
Janine Roth........................	Vice President of Business Development
Mark S. Smith....................	Vice President of Worldwide Sales
Chun P. Chui...................	Director
Michael L. Goguen.........	Director
Katherine M. Jen.............	Director
Frank J. Marshall.............	Director
Thomas F. Mendoza.......	Director
Victor E. Parker, Jr..........	Director

其中，董事会成员为：

Robert Thomas, 公司CEO

Feng Deng, 公司研发副总裁，创办人

Chun Chui, 代表投资机构

Michael Goguen, 代表投资机构Sequoia

Katherine Jen, 代表投资机构AsiaTech, Silicon Valley Equity Fund
Frank Marshall, 代表投资机构Big Basin
Thomas Mendoza, 代表投资机构
Victor Parker. 代表投资机构Spectrum

NetScreen公司员工规模

NetScreen的总部在硅谷的Sunnyvale。但到2004年，已经在世界各地都有了相应的分支机构或者代表处。

NetScreen期间，总部的地址，随着公司的不断发展壮大，总共搬迁过5次，从一个小作坊规模的初创公司，成长为一个在硅谷的高速237公路旁边有着高大上的办公大楼的，NASDAQ上市的，市值几十亿美金的公司。

NetScreen office locations throughout the years.

1. 355 W. Olive Avenue, Suite 101 — Sunnyvale
2. 4699 Old Ironsides Road — Sunnyvale
3. 2860 San Tomas Expressway — Sunnyvale
4. 350 Oakmead Parkway — Sunnyvale
5. 805 11th Ave, Bldg. 3, Ariba Campus — Sunnyvale

（NetScreen期间的5个总部地址）

公司IPO上市时是在第4个地方，350 Oakmead Parkway, Sunnyvale。后来搬到805 11th Ave， Bldg. 3, Sunnyvale处。

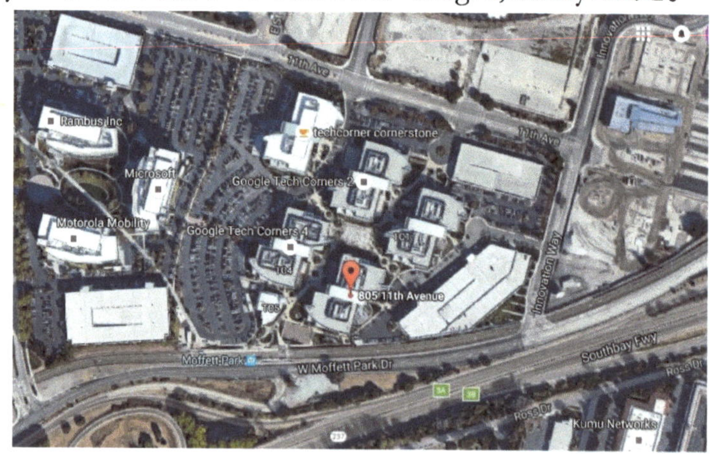

(NetScreen最后在Sunnyvale的总部地址)

NetScreen的团队大概分为管理团队（Exec），产品（PLM），研发（R&D），销售（Sales），市场（Marketing），运营（Operations）和人力（HR）。

1998年10月NetScreen Inc.员工为38人。32人为中国工程师。

1999年，NetScreen员工人数达 45人。

NetScreen上市的时候（2001年12月）， 有全职员工330人。 其中100人为研发人员。 47个销售和市场人员。 9个客户支持，和64位财务和后勤管理人员。

NetScreen在2002年9月30日的2002年度SEC 10K Filing报表中披露， 有全职员工493人。 其中149人是研发人员。 225人是销售市场人员；35人是客户支持， 84人为财务和后勤管理人员。

NetScreen在2003年9月30日的2003年度SEC 10K Filing报表中披露，其员工总数为646人。其中，181人是研发人员，277人是销售和市场人员，75个客户支持和113个财务和后勤管理人员。 2003年12月31日， NetScreen员工为859人。

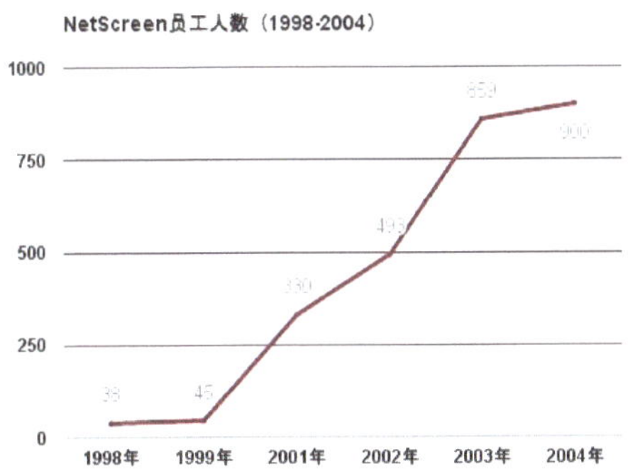

（NetScreen历年员工人数）

NetScreen在2004年4月被Juniper收购的时候，全球大概是900人。收购完成的时候，总共只有94名NetScreen员工因为位置重叠的原因被解雇。从上面数据可以看出，NetScreen在2001年上市之后并没有大面积的扩充公司规模，一直控制着员工人数。在2002年到2003年，员工人数有了一定规模的增长。在2004年被收购之前，公司规模一直是900人左右，支撑着一个市值为25亿美金的通信系统公司。是典型的一种美国高科技系统公司的运作方式，规模小但精悍能干。

第二章 资本内幕

NetScreen的创立，发展和上市，经历了典型的美国初创公司的各个历程，例如，天使和创投资本在各个阶段的投资。从1998年到2002年，NetScreen总共经历了A-F，共6轮的融资。
下图所示为NetScreen申请上市时S-1报表中公司主要股份持有者的股份分布：

Name of Beneficial Owner	Number of Shares Beneficially Owned	Percentage of Outstanding Shares Beneficially Owned: Before Offering	After Offering
Michael L. Goguen(1)	11,323,298	18.3%	%
Sequoia Capital and affiliates			
Sequoia Capital VII	9,164,056	14.8	
Victor E. Parker, Jr.(2)	4,754,177	7.7	
Spectrum Equity Investors and affiliates			
Spectrum Equity Investors IV, L.P.	4,670,978	7.5	
Feng Deng(3)	4,316,000	7.0	
Yan Ke(4)	4,196,000	6.8	
Qing Xie	3,482,666	5.6	
Robert D. Thomas(5)	2,795,000	4.5	
Katherine M. Jen(6)	1,566,664	2.5	
Silicon Valley Equity Fund and affiliates			
Mark S. Smith(7)	1,030,000	1.7	
David K. Flynn(8)	1,010,000	1.6	
Chun P. Chiu(9)	923,978	1.5	
Frank J. Marshall(10)	883,000	1.4	
Big Basin Partners L.P. and affiliates			
Charles R. Clark(11)	490,000	*	
James K. Gifford (12)	487,000	*	
Thomas F. Mendoza (13)	199,318	*	
All executive officers and directors as a group (16 persons)(14)	35,004,435	56.4	

（NetScreen申请上市时S-1报表中公司主要股份分布）

NetScreen上市的时候，经过各个阶段的股票稀释，三个创办人总共还持有19.4%的股份，其中，邓锋是整个NetScreen股本结构里作为个人占股最多的个人，为7%，依次为柯严，占股6.8%，谢青占股为5.6%。由于谢青已经在公司创办一年之后离开，所以，创办人在公司的整体股份结构上对应的投票权重只为13.8%。

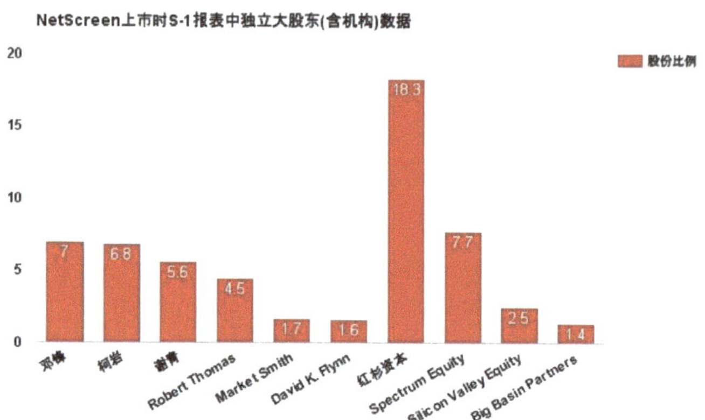

（NetScreen申请上市时S-1报表中公司主要股份分布）

在公司高管方面，1998年开始加入NetScreen并一直担任CEO的Robert Thomas占股为5.6%。销售副总裁Mark Smith占股为1.7%，市场副总裁David Flynn占股1.6%。

其他的股权基本上是分布在各个投资机构手里，其中红杉资本为最大的股东，占比18.3%。红杉资本的18.3%中，有14.8%是属于红杉资本的Sequoia Capital VII基金，其他的是Sequoia Capital and affiliates基金。

第二大机构股东是Spectrum Equlity，占股为7.7%。

公司的所有高管团队，董事会成员（所代表的基金）的股票总算占NetScreen的56.4%。

在融资方面，NetScreen上市时流通股票为7千百万股，经历过A，B，C，D和E轮的融资。

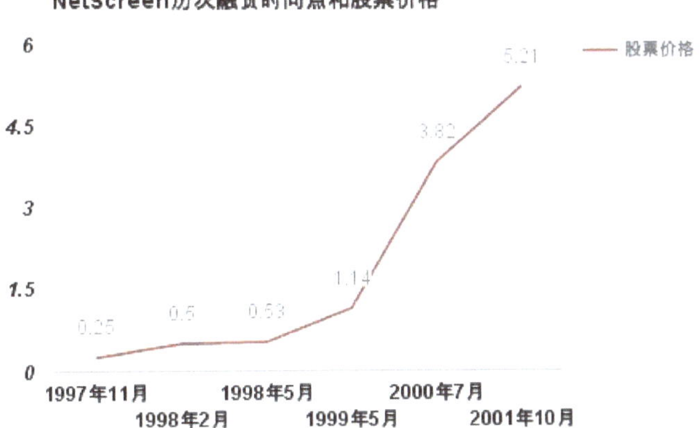

(NetScreen历次融资时间点和股票价格)

A轮融资：

1997年11月到1998年1月，NetScreen以每股25美分价格，出售4百40万股票。

B轮融资：

1998年2月，NetScreen以每股50美分价格出售2百万股票。

C轮融资：

1998年5月，NetScreen以每股53美分价格出售7百万股票。

D轮融资：

1999年5月，NetScreen以1.14美金价格出售9百49万股票。

E轮融资：

2000年7月和8月，NetScreen以3.82美金价格出售9百57万股票。

F轮融资：

2001年10月，NetScreen以5.21美金价格出售5百76万股票。

创办人股权结构：

NetScreen创立的时候，三个创办人每人发行了1百万股票；给未来的员工留了2百万股票。所以总共是5百万股票。

三个创办人业余时间做了一年的原型系统，在开始融资一百万美金的时候，公司投后的定价为5百万美金。 第一个一百万美金获得了NetScreen公司20%的股份。
在上市之前的几年，NetScreen公司的股票经历了2次2：1的分拆。所以，也可以理解为最开始的一股变为4股。
换言之，1997年10月，公司发行1千2百万股票给3个创办人。每人4百万股。其中2百4十万 股票是立刻归属创办人完全拥有。另外的1百2十万股在公司成立6个月后归属创办人。公司创办1年后（1998年10月），另外的1百2十万股归属创办人。
换言之，在1998年10月，每个创办人获得了160万NetScreen的股票。创办人股票是按照36个月，每个月2.77%的比例获得。
由于Ken Xie在1999年9月离开NetScreen，NetScreen董事会对Ken Xie股票的处理是加速了他1百万股票，和回购了剩下的73万股股票。
截止到2001年6月30日，3个创办人的股票总数为1千2百万股。
Feng Deng.................................... 4,316,000
Yan Ke.. 4,196,000
Qing Xie.. 3,482,666

流通股的变化

在1998年的8月，董事会做了一次2:1的股权分裂。每股变2股。1999年4月，再做了一下2:1分裂。2000年11月，再一次做了一个2:1分裂。
换言之，如果1997年的1股，到2000年的11月，成为4股。

投资机构/人:

NetScreen从1997年创办到2001年上市的期间，经历了天使，A轮，B轮和C轮的几次大的机构融资。
其中，最大的机构和天使投资人分别为：红杉资本占股为(18.3%)，Spectrum Equity(7.7%)， Silicon Valley Equity Fund(2.5%)，Chun Chiu(1.53%)， Big Basin Partners(1.4%)。

NetScreen在上市前，由于各轮资本融资的进入，有了许多大大小小的投资人（机构），其中要特别注意的是，投资机构里包括了之后以41亿美金收购NetScreen的Juniper Networks。

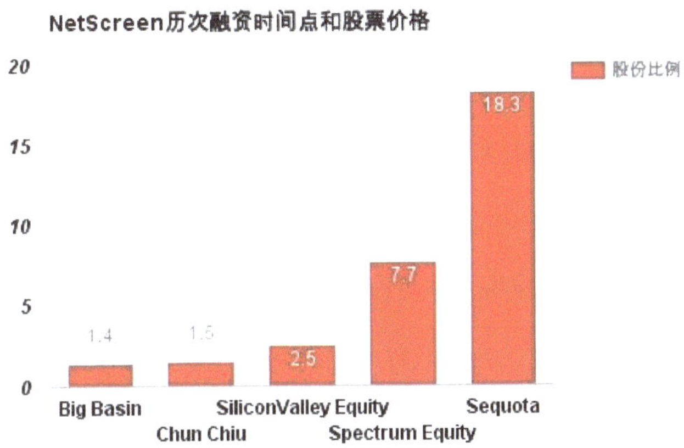

(NetScreen股本结构中机构占股分布)

附录1是NetScreen投资人和机构的完整列表。许多后期的投资人，特别是基金，都是NetScreen在IPO路演时认购的投资人或者机构。后期吸收的一些投资基本上是单纯的财务投资。不太具备战略意义。

第三章 研发探究

NetScreen的研发是在邓锋，柯严领导下的华人工程师为主体的一个团队。研发速度非常快。执行力非常强。这是NetScreen作为一个以中国人为主体的系统公司能在硅谷生存下来的重要原因之一。

邓锋负责公司的研发团队，主要职能部门分为硬件部门，软件ScreenOS部门，新产品预研部门和QA测试部门。
其中邓锋自己长期兼任硬件部门的负责人。硬件部门主要分为ASIC芯片部门和平台Platform部门。Raymond Wei是ASIC部门的负责人。Platform平台部门主要负责Board和System设计，Jackson Tong是负责人。
ScreenOS部门的负责人是Roger Lian。ScreenOS部门在不同的时期有不同的组。每个组是一个经理，例如，Flow团队，Network团队Changming Liu是负责人，ALG团队，VPN团队Michael Shieh是负责人等。
测试部门按照ScreenOS的模块有相应的团队。测试部门的负责人是Ting Tan 。内部按照测试的分工分为若干个组。QA测试部门也包括客户支持团队。
柯严作为创办人之一，出任公司软件部分的总架构师并直接领导一个Advanced Tecnology Group。ATG有点类似CTO Office的性质，是NetScreen新产品的实验基地，包括ASIC功能架构设计(与ASIC部门合作)和验证， Kernel改造和研发(与ScreenOS部门合作)。通常ATG把下一代产品作出原型后，转移给ScreenOS团队做产品化。ATG的负责人是Yuming Mao。

NetScreen在上市后，成功的收购了两家安全产品公司。分别是IDS公司OneSecure和SSL/VPN公司Neoteris。 NetScreen的IDP/IPS的积累， SSL/VPN产品线基本上来自上述两个公司。

Unique Solution & Technology Platform

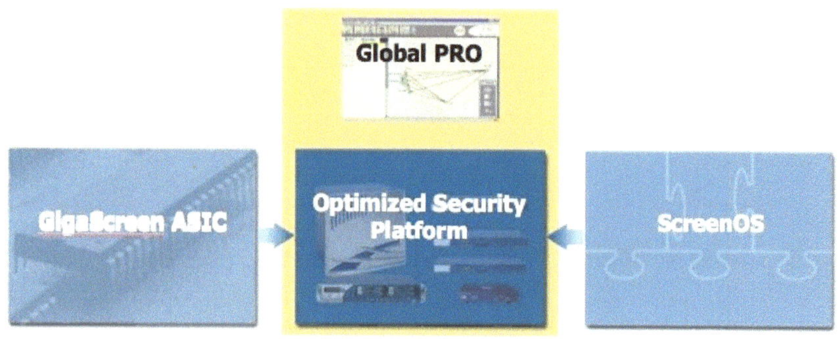

（NetScreen产品布局图）

NetScreen从产品研发的角度是一个系统公司，其ASIC，ScreenOS和管理软件Global Pro部门被集成体现在NetScreen Appliances的整体解决方案中，并被广泛应用在运营商，企业网和SOHO市场。

NetScreen的产品由于其高效稳定，获得了各种评测机构，客户的广泛欢迎，并获得了许多荣誉。下图是其获得的一些相关荣誉清单。

<u>NetScreen荣誉榜</u>

通常而言，NetScreen的产品分高中低端产品。其中ISG2000/1000，NS5400/5200，NS1000算高端产品线。NS500算中端产品线。NS200/100/50和其他算低端产品线。其中产品系列500以上的都带有NetScreen自研的ASIC芯片，例如加密芯片。5200以上还带有IPSEC/VPN ASIC。全部属于自己研发的系统。系统软件都是自研的ScreenOS。(注：后来研发的SRX5800是开始基于JUNOS的软件。)

NetScreen对研发的投入一直很大，其中：

1998年是2百30万美金。公司全年收入为6百万美金。

1999年是1千5百80万美金。公司全年营收为5百80万美金。

2000年是1千4百万美金，占总营收的52.8%。

2001年是2千5百60万美金，占总营收的29.9%。

2002年的研发投入是3千2百80万美金，为总营收的23.6%。

2003年研发投入是4千3百90万美金，为总营收的17.8%。

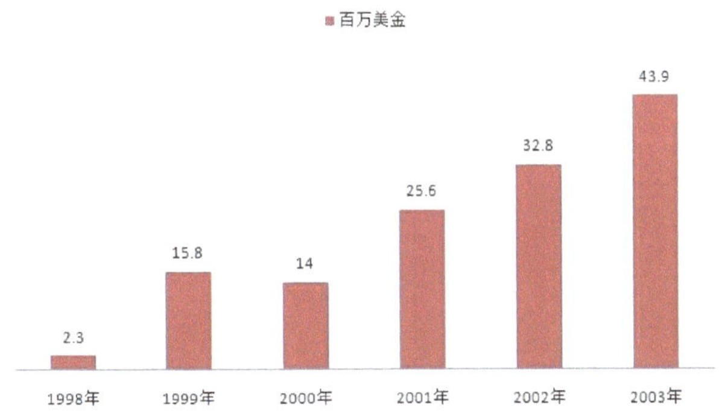

NetScreen的研发的显著特点是执行力强。产品推出的速度非常快。下面是NetScreen期间产品的发布时间表。可以很容易的看

出，在2001年和2002年，产品推出的节奏非常紧密。2005年NetScreen被Juniper收购之后，产品发布的节奏明显放缓。

从1998年到2009年，NetScreen产品系列总共发布产品17次。下面是各个产品发布的详细时间点和相应的产品型号的考据：

1998年6月，NetScreen推出NetScreen-100和NetScreen-10网络安全产品。
1999年9月，NetScreen推出NetScreen-5网络安全产品。
2000年5月，NetScreen推出基于GigaScreen ASIC NetScreen 1000网络安全产品。
2001年5月，NetScreen推出NetScreen-500网络安全产品。
2001年6月，NetScreen推出NetScreen-5XP网络安全产品。
2001年11月，NetScreen推出NetScreen-25/50网络安全产品。
2002年1月，NetScreen推出NetScreen-204/208网络安全产品。
2002年4月15日，NetScreen推出基于GigaScreen ASIC II的NetScreen 5200网络安全产品。
2002年9月，NetScreen推出NetScreen Remote网络安全产品。
2002年9月，NetScreen推出NetScreen-IDP 100网络安全产品。
2002年10月，NetScreen推出GigaScreen ASIC II Based NetScreen-5400网络安全产品。
2002年11月，NetScreen推出NetScreen-IDP 500网络安全产品。
2004年4月16日，NetScreen宣布推出基于GigaScreen-III ASIC ISG2000产品。
2005年5月9日，Juniper SPG宣布推出基于GigaScreen III ASIC ISG2000+IDP和ISG1000产品。
2008年9月15日, Juniper发布世界上最高端的防火墙系统SRX 5800系列。
2009年3月9日, Juniper发布SRX 3000系列。

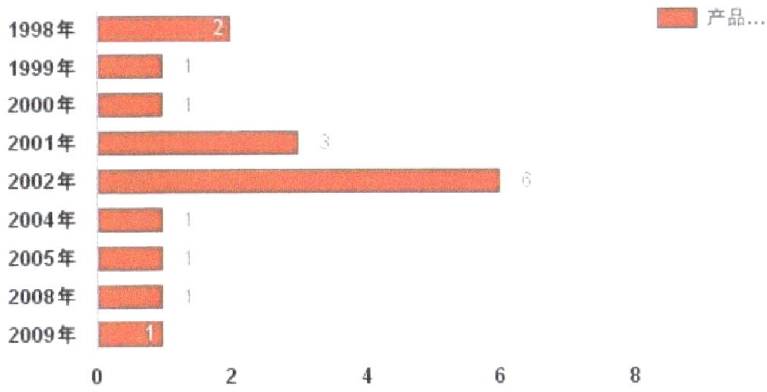

（NetScreen产品系列发布时间点分布图）

NetScreen产品系列发布时间点（1998-2009）

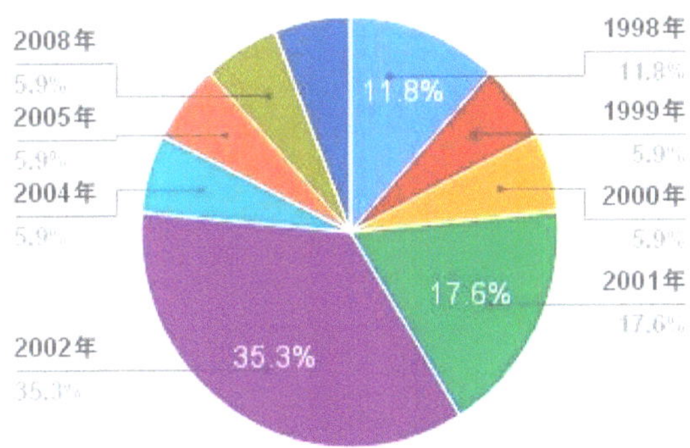

（NetScreen产品系列发布时间点分布图）

从分析统计的数据可见，上市之前和之后的第一年，即2001年和2002年，是NetScreen发布产品的最高峰，分别为17.6%和35.3%。是NetScreen研发最活跃的两年。

下面所列的图集是NetScreen在合并入Juniper之前的产品系列图。Juniper收购NetScreen之后产生的产品线属于SRX系列，没有列出在这里。

总体而言，NetScreen在2004年初，通过其快速的研发能力，灵活多变的企业网战略，形成了高，中和低端的各个产品线。其中，其NS5000， ISG2000系列是NetScreen的旗舰产品。

ISG2000/1000

NS5400/5200

NS1000

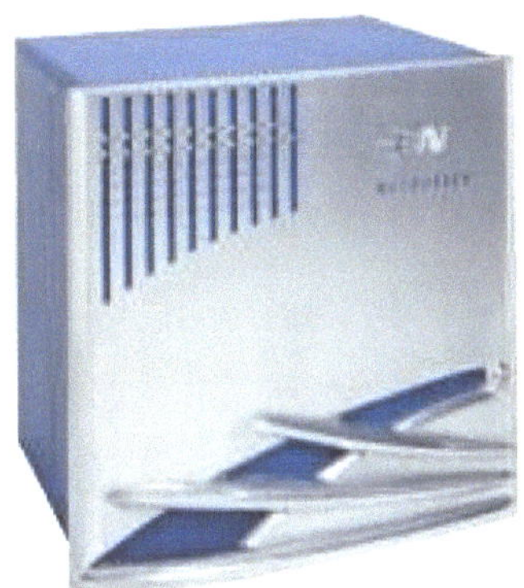

NS500

NS200

NetScreen - 204

NetScreen - 208

NS100

NS50

NetScreen-50 and NetScreen-25

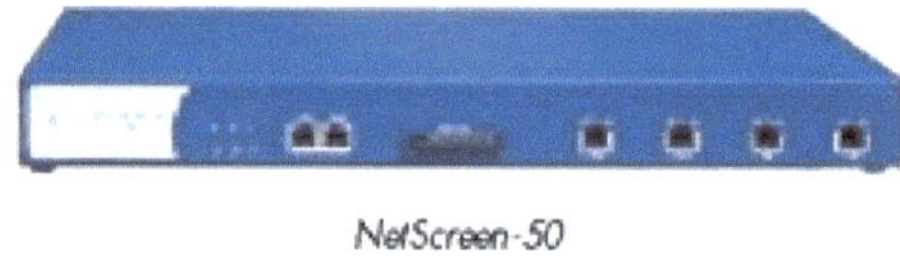

NetScreen-50

NetScreen-25

NS5xt/g

NetScreen的ASIC芯片：

NetScreen公司的主要创新点是通过硬件芯片（ASIC和FPGA）的网络安全加速解决方案。所以，其自主研发的ASIC芯片研发是公司产品解决方案里最重要的一个组成部分。

在NetScreen独立发展的6年里，总共经过了4次ASIC的芯片设计流片，分别是：

1999年12月13日，NetScreen发布了其第一个Gigabit性能的ASIC芯片的流片成功,并引起了工业界的广泛关注.

"SANTA CLARA, Calif., Dec. 13(1999) /PRNewswire/ -- NetScreen Technologies, a leading developer of ASIC-based Internet security appliances and systems, announced today that it has completed development of the industry's first Gigabit performance security ASIC. The GigaScreen ASIC is NetScreen's second generation security acceleration ASIC that delivers a "Triple Crown" of security industry firsts, including: the first Gigabit performance IPSec encryption, the first silicon-based stateful inspection firewall, and the first silicon to combine encryption, authentication, PKI and firewall acceleration in a single chip. This technology breakthrough drives critical security functions into silicon to achieve unprecedented performance levels.

The GigaScreen ASIC will power a new generation of NetScreen Internet security appliances and systems, the first of which will be available in Q1 2000."

GigaScreen ASIC在当时是第一个防火墙加速的ASIC芯片，主要是包含一些加密算法的引擎，例如，1.2Gbps的DES, 400Mbps的3DES，MD5和Sha-1等。

"The GigaScreen ASIC's three industry firsts will enable NetScreen to achieve breakthrough performance levels in VPN and firewall security applications. These three firsts are:

-- First Gigabit performance IPSec encryption engine -- more than twice the performance of leading merchant silicon. The GigaScreen ASIC's encryption engine delivers 1.2 Gbps DES encryption and 400 Mbps 3DES IPSec encryption with or without simultaneous authentication. The authentication acceleration engine supports both the MD5 and SHA-1 algorithms.

-- First silicon-based stateful inspection firewall, including TCP/IP header parsing, stateful inspection session lookup, Gigabit throughput network address translation (NAT) and a flexible policy search engine capable of searching 25 million policies per second.

-- First silicon to integrate encryption, authentication, PKI and firewall acceleration into a single chip."

2000年5月，NeteScreen发布了GigaScreen ASIC的第二代芯片。

2001年6月，NetScreen完成并推出第二代GigaScreen-II ASIC。GigaScreen-II芯片是第二代芯片。IPSEC/VPN的报文在通过主CPU建立会话(Session)后，可以用GigaScreen-II芯片来处理。这个重大的芯片加速方案极大的提高了高端防火墙的性能。

2002年4月15日，NetScreen推出基于GigaScreen ASIC II NetScreen 5200网络安全产品。在高端防火墙市场上获得了很大的成功。

GigaScreen-II ASIC Technology

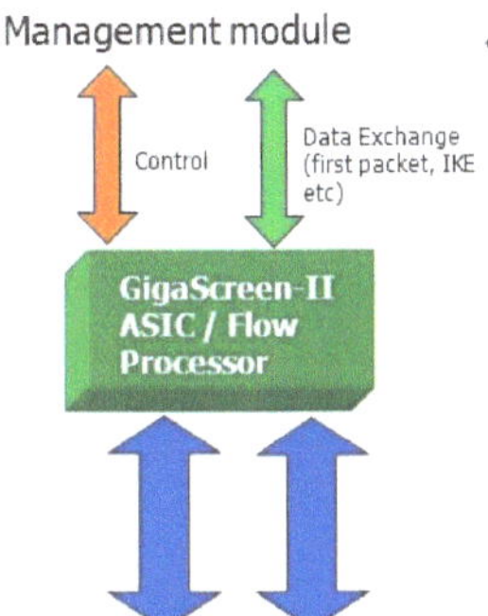

- GigaScreen-II is a security processor
  - Breakthrough performance
    - 2 Gbps firewall; 1 Gbps VPN
  - Massive scalability
    - Linear scalability when connected to a switched backplane
  - Complete security processing
    - Complete packet processing with little to no CPU intervention
  - Programmability
    - Ability to add packet classification and content inspection engines

（NetScreen基于ASIC芯片的高端产品体系结构）

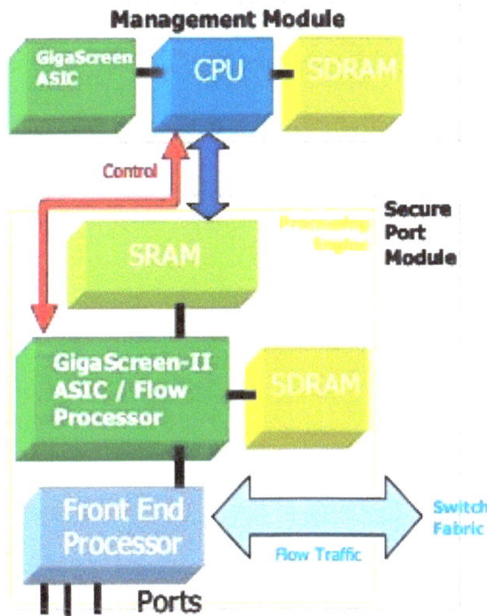

（NetScreen基于ASIC芯片的高端产品体系结构）

2003年10月，NetScreen完成并推出第三代GigaScreen-III ASIC。并应用在ISG2000系统中。ISG2000之后成为NetScreen/Juniper网络安全产品线的旗舰产品。

在NetScreen的6年过程中，历经了GigaScreen，GigaScreen-II，GigaScreenIII的研发和流片。其中最为惋惜的是：

GigaScreenIII-X完成了所有的研发工作，但在Juniper期间被停止，没有大规模流片和投入使用。这个战略性的叫停对于NetScreen ASIC的研发和整个NetScreen的产品线布局是一个分水岭，严重延缓了NetScreen产品线过去快速敏捷的节奏，直接导致了竞争公司，例如，Fortinet和后续其他公司的崛起。后来的事实证明，放弃基于ASIC为基础的NetScreen产品的战略是严重错误的，打乱了NetScreen的产品布局。

（NetScreen GigaScreen II芯片和处理卡）

NetScreen市场突破的亮点就是通过ASIC加速的方式，构建高性能的网络安全产品。Juniper轻易的放弃了这个制高点，并在未来的市场竞争中教训惨重，并丢失了许多市场份额。这对企业产品的高科技公司在M&A后处理集成和整合都是一个很好的经验教训。

（NetScreen GigaScreen III芯片）

（基于NetScreen GigaScreen III芯片的数据卡）

（NetScreen GigaScreen III-X芯片）

NetScreen ScreenOS

NetScreen是一个系统公司，其核心是ScreenOS操作系统，把硬件，ASIC芯片，CPU主板上的其他控制逻辑有机的联合在一起，提供一个具备网络交换，路由，安全的一个系统设备。

ScreenOS是一个自研的通信操作系统，不是基于Linux，也非BSD系列。存在着一些早期监控系统Nucleus RTOS的痕迹。但基本上被重写，特别是ScreenOS 5.0之后，做了一个非常大鳄改造。ScreenOS基本上形成了一个POSIX-Like的RTOS，具备了POSIX 1.b和1.c的不少特征，例如，调度，同步，Timer和包括对ASMP多CPU的支持。

在CPU目标的支持上，逐步自研增加了多种MIPS CPU(5K和7K)，PowerPC(405/750/7447)，xScale/ARM等的目标支持。在MM内存管理部分，已经具备基于MMU保护的各种粒度的虚存管理，而且为了嵌入式系统的考虑，完整了考虑了各种Cache和TLB Miss带来的性能损失。

在分布式系统方面，ScreenOS已经能够与QNX的Neutrino的微内核互通，并成功的实现了ScreenOS远程boot基于QNX的IDP处理卡的并行体系结构(ISG2000+IDP)产品中。

在网络部分，通过与第三方合作，加上自研的集成，基本上具备了完整的动态路由的各种协议，例如，对BGP，OSPF的支持。也具备了HA的Active/Active，Active/Standby的支持。

在安全部分，是自研ScreenOS的主要成分，例如基于虚拟vsys的FW，VPN等。经过多年打磨，ScreenOS已经是一个很完整的具备防火墙功能，VPN功能和各种ALG功能的网络安全操作系统。另外，ScreenOS也逐步增加了GPRS等许多其他功能，支持无线核心网的网络安全系统。

在2004年初，ScreenOS已经发展为基本上可以非常容易的与POSIX OS对接和互相移植的状态。而且已经启动Linux的移植计划。例如，把ScreenOS作为一个完整的进程运行在Linux的用户态上。下图所示是ScreenOS操作系统对一个网络数据报文的处理流程：

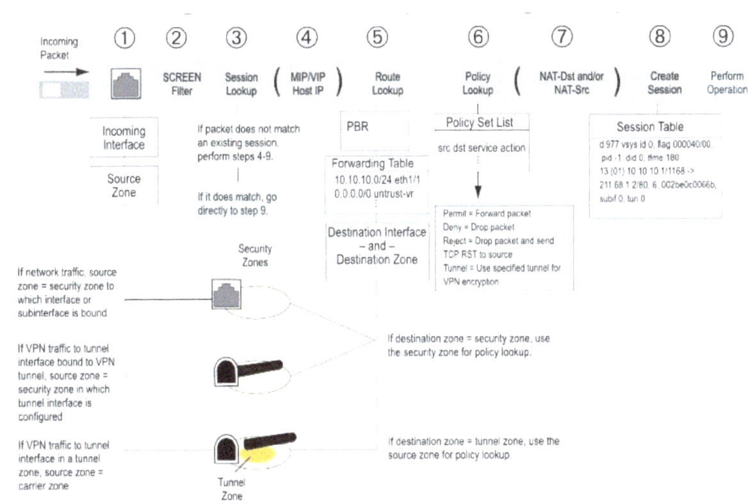

（NetScreen ScreenOS体系结构图）

ScreenOS在Juniper收购后，持续发布到2009年ScreenOS 6.3，然后就停止了研发，进入了维护状态。

其历年的发布路标总结如下：

2000年5月4日，NetScreen发布ScreenOS操作系统2.0。
2000年9月18日，NetScreen发布ScreenOS操作系统2.1。
2000年12月18日，NetScreen发布ScreenOS操作系统2.5。
2001年4月30日，NetScreen发布ScreenOS操作系统2.6。
2001年9月10日，NetScreen发布ScreenOS操作系统2.7。
2001年10月1日，NetScreen发布ScreenOS操作系统3.0。
2001年12月28日，NetScreen发布ScreenOS操作系统2.8。
2002年1月2日，NetScreen发布ScreenOS操作系统3.1。
2002年8月1日，NetScreen发布ScreenOS操作系统4.0。
2003年12月18日，NetScreen发布ScreenOS操作系统5.。.
2004年10月22日，Juniper SPG 发布ScreenOS操作系统5.1。
2005年5月11日，Juniper SPG 发布ScreenOS操作系统5.2。
2005年10月24日，Juniper SPG发布ScreenOS操作系统5.3。
2006年7月24日，Juniper SPG发布ScreenOS操作系统5.4。
2007年4月19日，Juniper发布ScreenOS 6.0。
2008年1月28日，Juniper发布ScreenOS 6.1。
2008年11月7日，Juniper发布ScreenOS 6.2。
2009年9月1日，Juniper发布ScreenOS 6.3。

ScreenOS总共历经18个正式的对外发布版本。其中ScreenOS 5.0是NetScreen公司创办以来最大的一次全面调整，历时1年多。为后续高端系统，特别是ISG2000产品线打下了基础。

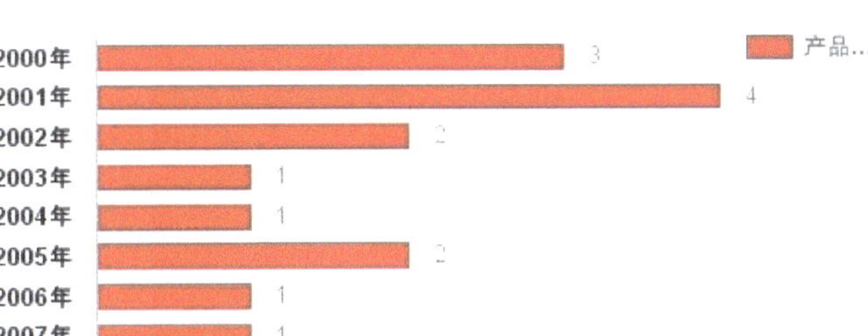

（NetScreen ScreenOS历年发布分布图）

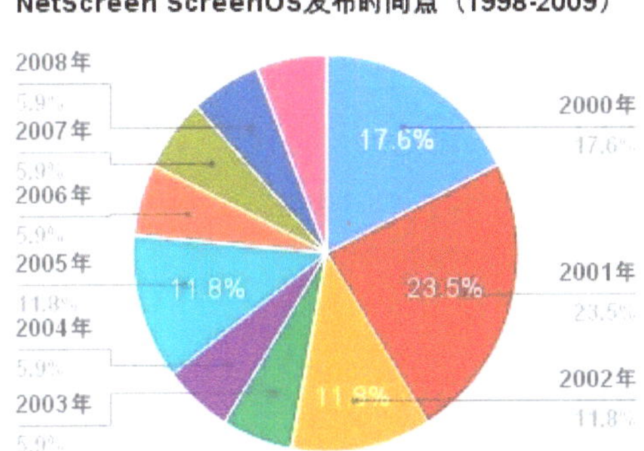

（NetScreen ScreenOS历年发布分布图）

在上述18个发布中， 2000年占17.6% 2001年占23.5% 2002年占11.8% 2003年占5.9% 2004年占5.9% 2005年11.8% 2006年占5.9% 2007年占5.9% 2008年占5.9% 2009年占5.9%

从统计可见，2000年和2001年是ScreenOS发布最大版本的时间段，分别为17.6%和23.5%。另外，我们可以发现，ScreenOS的发布与系统的发布的时基本上间段是一致的。都分布在2001和2002年时间段。

NetScreen的专利

NetScreen上市的时候，已经批准的专利为3个。覆盖了NetSCreen的主要核心技术。下面是NetScreen的S-1报表中关于NetScreen专利的介绍：

“Our success and ability to compete are substantially dependent upon our internally developed technology and know-how. **We have three patent applications and one provisional patent application pending in the United States relating to the design of our products.** We have elected to extend one of these patent applications to other countries. Our engineering teams have significant expertise in ASIC design, and we own the rights to the design of the ASIC that forms the core of our products. Our ScreenOS operating system and applications and our NetScreen-Global PRO and NetScreen-Global Manager software were developed internally and are protected by United States and international copyright laws.”

NetScreen几个最重要专利的简单介绍如下：

United States Patent 6,701,432

Firewall including local bus

Inventors:Deng; Feng (San Jose, CA), Ke; Yan (San Jose, CA), Luo; Dongping (Milpitas, CA) Assignee:Netscreen Technologies, Inc. (Sunnyvale, CA)

Filed:April 1, 1999

United States Patent 6,772,347

Method, apparatus and computer program product for a network firewall

Inventors:Xie; Ken (Atherton, CA), Ke; Yan (San Jose, CA), Mao; Yuming (Milpitas, CA) Assignee:Juniper Networks, Inc. (Sunnyvale, CA)

Filed:April 1, 1999

United States Patent 7,093,280

Internet security system

Inventors: Ke; Yan (San Jose, CA), Mao; Yuming (Milpitas, CA), Xu; Wilson (Cupertino, CA), Leu; Brian Yean-Shiang (San Jose, CA)

Assignee: Juniper Networks, Inc. (Sunnyvale, CA)

Filed: September 27, 2001

2004年，NetScreen并入Juniper Networks公司之后，所有的专利技术也变成Juniper Networks的专利。后来这些专利技术成为Juniper Networks起诉PaloAlto Networks侵犯核心专利的主要起诉依据之一。

Juniper起诉PaloAlto Networks时总共用了如下6个专利：

7,302,700: "Method and apparatus for implementing a layer 3/layer 7 firewall in an L2 device" by Mao et. al. and assigned to Juniper Networks, Inc.. **Filed 9/28/2001** & Granted 11/27/2007.

6,772,347: "Method, apparatus and computer program product for a network firewall" by Xie et. al. and assigned to Juniper Networks, Inc.. **Filed 3/15/2000** & Granted 8/3/2004.

7,650,634: "Intelligent integrated network security device" by Zuk and assigned to Juniper Networks, Inc.. **Filed 3/28/2003** & Granted 1/19/2010.

7,093,280: "Internet security system" by Ke et. al. and assigned to Juniper Networks, Inc.. **Filed 9/27/2001** & Granted 8/15/2006.

8,077,723: "Packet processing in a multiple processor system" by Zuk et. al. and assigned to Juniper Networks, Inc.. **Filed 5/14/2010** & Granted 12/13/2011.

7,779,459: "Method and apparatus for implementing a layer 3/layer 7 firewall in an L2 device" by Mao et. al. and assigned to Juniper Networks, Inc.. **Filed 10/9/2007** & Granted 8/17/2010.

第四章 财务分析

NetScreen的财务分析

NetScreen创办于1997年10月。1998年开始销售其防火墙产品并产生营收。 营收额基本上保持了年度60%的高速增长。到准备上市申报S1文件时，营业额已经达到6千万美金。下图是NetScreen在上市时的财务一览。

Summary Consolidated Financial Data
(in thousands, except per share amounts)

	Period From October 30, 1997 (Inception) to September 30, 1998	Year Ended September 30, 1999	2000	2001
Consolidated Statement of Operations Data:				
Total revenues	$ 665	$ 5,871	$ 26,584	$ 85,563
Gross margin	476	4,183	18,209	59,767
Loss from operations	(3,822)	(19,810)	(33,478)	(32,223)
Net loss	(3,758)	(19,730)	(33,021)	(31,305)
Deemed dividend on Series E redeemable convertible preferred stock	--	--	(699)	(2,923)
Net loss applicable to common stockholders	(3,758)	(19,730)	(33,720)	(34,228)
Net loss per share applicable to common stockholders:				
Basic and diluted	$ (1.22)	$ (2.99)	$ (2.82)	$ (2.05)
Weighted average shares--basic and diluted	3,079	6,598	11,954	16,696
Pro forma net loss per share applicable to common stockholders:				
Basic and diluted				$ (0.70)
Weighted average shares--basic and diluted				49,169

在2001年全年，NetScreen营收达到8千5百万美金。 NetScreen在2002年突破了1亿3千8百万美金营收。2003年收入为245M美金，即2.45亿美金。

2004年Juniper Networks收购NetScreen的时候， NetScreen的客户从运营商到企业客户大概有850家，遍布全球。公司在03年开始赢利，并有3.7亿美金的现金储备， 公司市值高达24亿美金。 设备装机量高达30万。

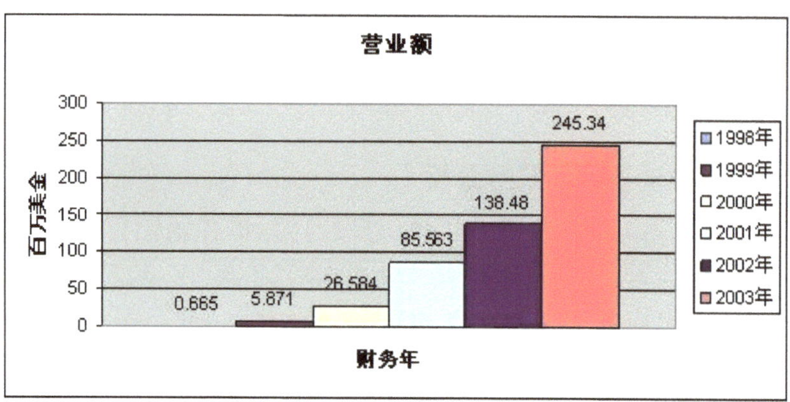

(NetScreen上市前历年的营业额)

NetScreen强健的公司基础一览：

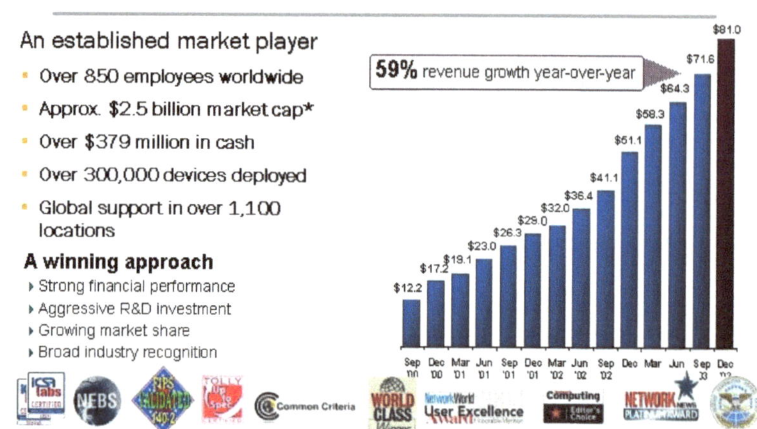

(NetScreen公司业务成长概貌)

NetScreen Firewall/VPN产品市场分额图解与比较

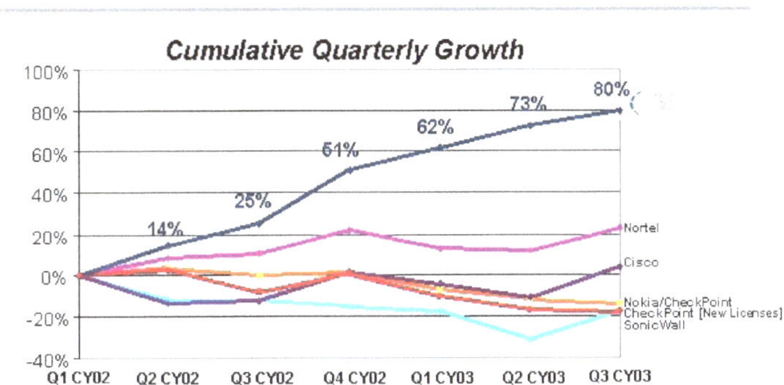

"NetScreen continues to gain market share from its competition further validating its purpose-built, hardware-based approach to integrated firewall and VPN solutions."

Jeff Wilson, Infonetics Research, July 2003

Product revenue growth rate indexed from Q1 2002. Based on FW/VPN appliance and software product revenues as reported by Infonetics research and publicly available company filings

(NetScreen公司历年的营收季度成长)

NetScreen的毛利率（Gross Margin）一直是70%多，在通信设备厂商方面财务很健康的。在2003年公司开始迅速增长，接近80%，并达到1.89亿美金。在2001年上市的时候，毛利率才是5千9百万美金。

下面是从财务的多维角度对NetScreen从1998年到2004年左右的财务状况的深度剖析，其中包括了历年的毛利，毛利率，净收入，销售与市场的开销，总营收开销等数据。从中可以一窥NetScreen发展中的各个阶段的财务状况。

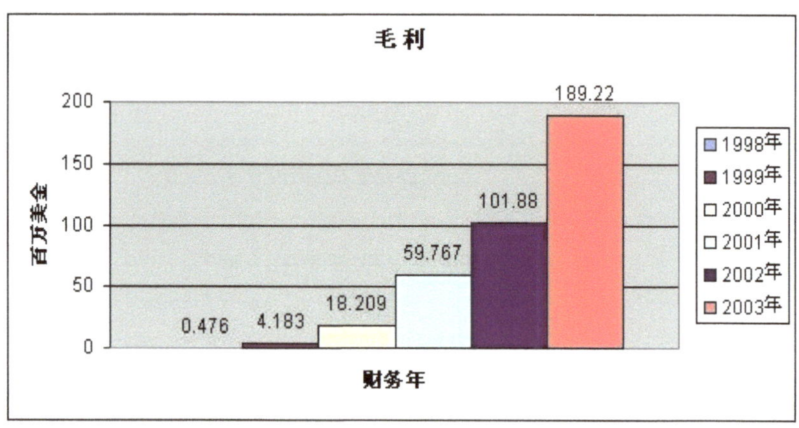

(NetScreen公司历年的营收毛利)

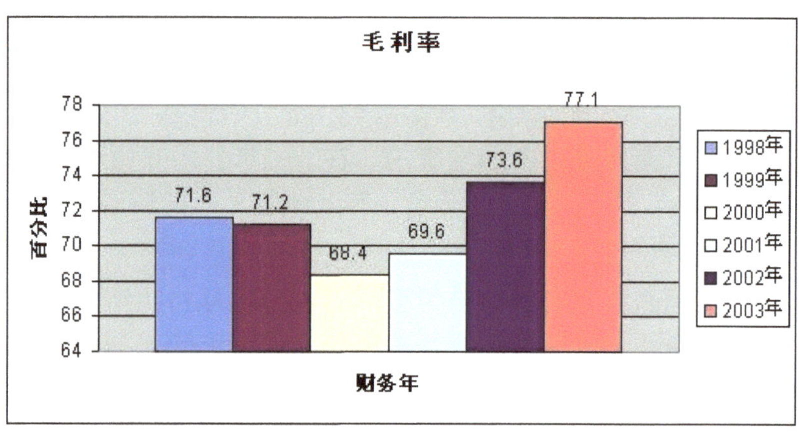

(NetScreen公司历年的营收毛利率)

NetScreen在2003年开始盈利，之前一直是在增长市场份额。2003年公司盈利5千1百万美金。

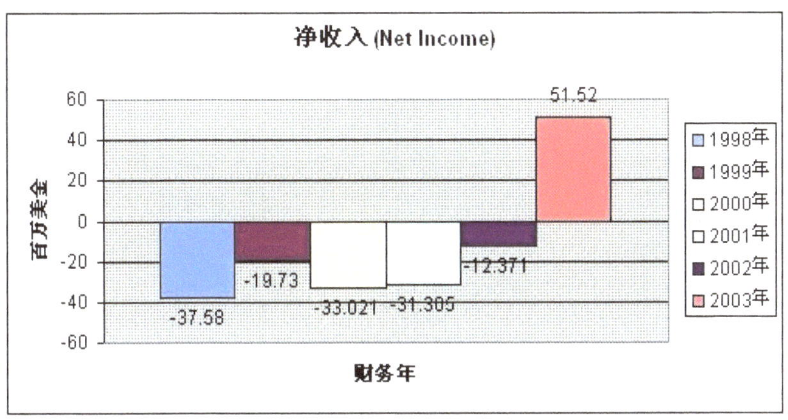

(NetScreen公司历年的净收入)

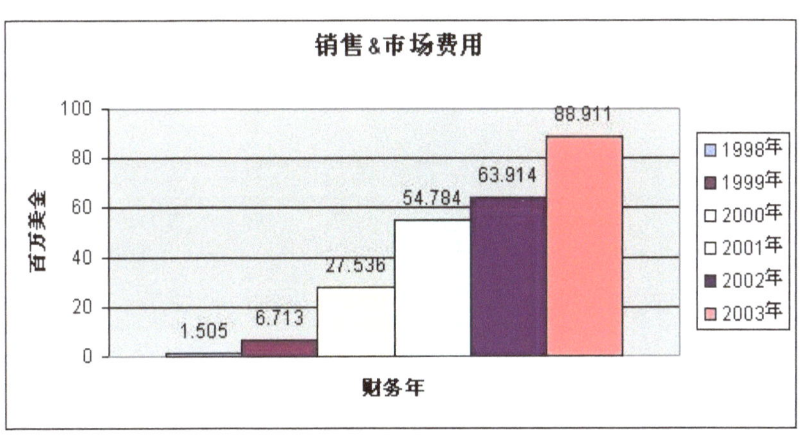

(NetScreen公司历年的销售和市场开销)

NetScreen在销售和市场费用开销方面一直控制的不错。在公司创办初期的1998，1999年，销售和市场开销很少。在2001年左右，随着各种产品的不断推出，和成功IPO，扩大了销售和市场费用。

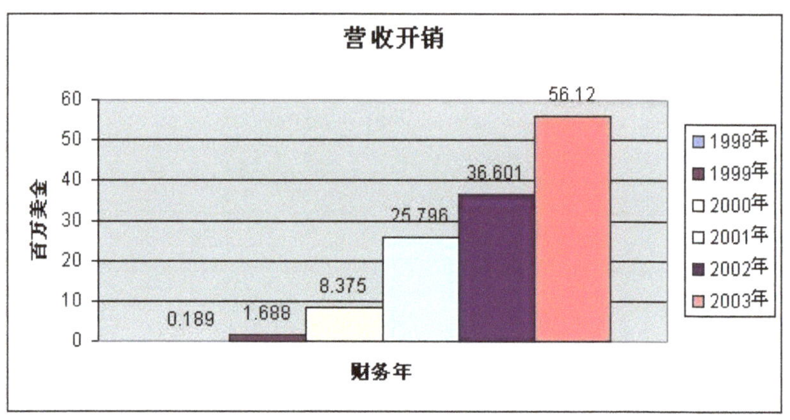

(NetScreen公司历年的营收开销)

下图为NetScreen与Juniper当年的市值， 2003年的营收，公司现金的对比。

Individual Company Facts	Juniper	NetScreen
Market Cap	$11.5 Billion	$2.4Bn
Revenue CY2003	$701.4 Million	$275.2 Million
Cash	$1.0 Billion	$378 Million

从上面的数据可见，NetScreen在2003年底的市值是大约24亿美金，2003年营业额为2.75亿美金。公司账户里有3.78亿现金。

NetScreen的销售模式

NetScreen的安全产品主要是网络防火墙， 入侵检测设备和IPSEC和SSL VPN设备和服务。客户主要是运营商市场和企业市场。

2003年财年，NetScreen的年度报表中声称其对运营商市场主要是通过直销的手段；对企业市场的销售主要是通过批发商和分销商的方式。通过渠道的销售产生的营业收入占总收入的

92.1%。在2003年10，11，12三个月，这个数据是89.4%。2002年，这个比例是86.9%。

NetScreen在1998年--2003年的5年里，防火墙和VPN业务的产品销售的数字大概如下：
1998年 64万美金
1999年 5百66万美金
2000年 2千3百40万美金
2001年 7千1百20万美金
2002年 1亿1千1百30万美金，比2001年增长60%
2003年 2亿零40万美金，比2002年增长75.8%

NetScreen在NASDAQ的表现

NetScreen是在2001年10月5日正式向美国证券委员会提交S－1上市申请材料的。在同年的12月12日上市。公司股票代号NSCN。

下面是公司当时在NASDAQ的官方信息。

Company Name NETSCREEN TECHNOLOGIES INC Company Address 805 11TH AVENUE BUILDING 3 SUNNYVALE, CA 94089

Company Phone (408) 543-2100

Company Website www.netscreen.com

CEO Robert D. Thomas

Employees (as of 9/30/2001) 330 （员工数）

State of Inc DE

Fiscal Year End 9/30

Status Priced (12/12/2001)

Proposed Symbol NSCN

Exchange NASDAQ

Share Price $16.00 （股票的定价）

Shares Offered 10,000,000 （公开发行1千万股股票）

Offer Amount $160,000,000.00

Total Expenses $2,000,000.00

Shares Over Alloted 0

Shareholder Shares Offered -- Shares Outstanding 72,016,326 （公司总共的流通股票）

Lockup Period (days) 180 （锁定时间）

Lockup Expiration 6/10/2002 （解锁时间）

Quiet Period Expiration 1/7/2002

CIK 0001088454

NSCN开盘第一天 ,股票开盘价位$23.76,收盘价位于$23.14。总交易量达 6 百万股。公司市 值为17亿美金。

之后，NetScreen的股票经历了在NASDAQ市场上589天的公开交易。公司市值基本上维持在25亿美金左右。

2004年2月9日,全球第二大网络通讯设备公司 Juniper Networks. 以NetScreen 股票NSCN 2月6日市值26.40美金为基点,出价约40亿美金并购NetScreen,引 起了全球通讯和安全市场的巨大轰动,

2004年4月12日是NetScreen的股票NSCN的最后一个成交日。历时589天。

下面图表是NSCN在各个时期在NASDAQ的数据图表。以做历史研究之用。

（NetScreen NSCN股票走势图）

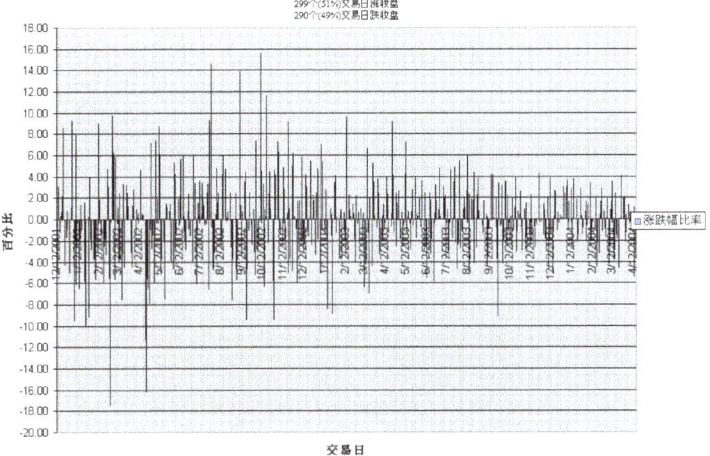

（NetScreen NSCN股票跌幅图）

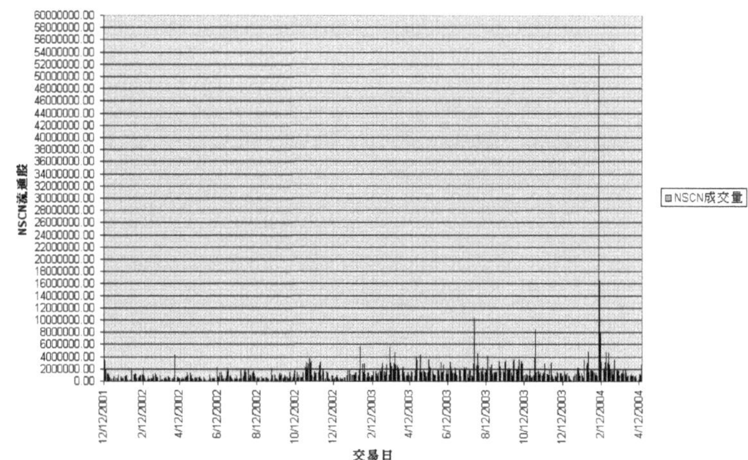

（NetScreen NSCN股票成交量图）

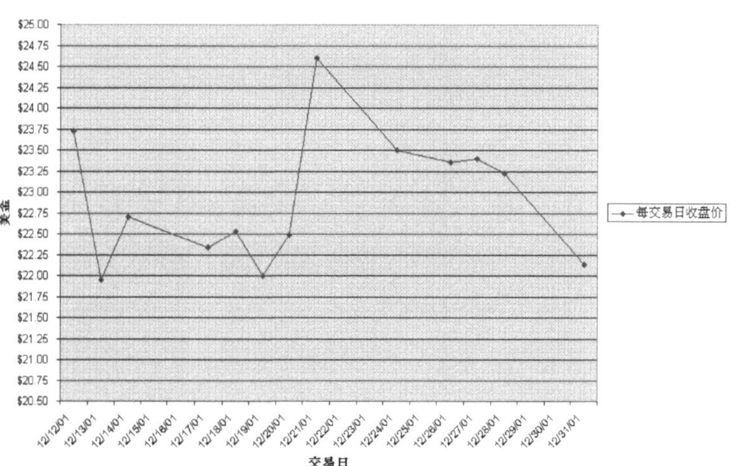

（NetScreen NSCN 2001年价格走势图）

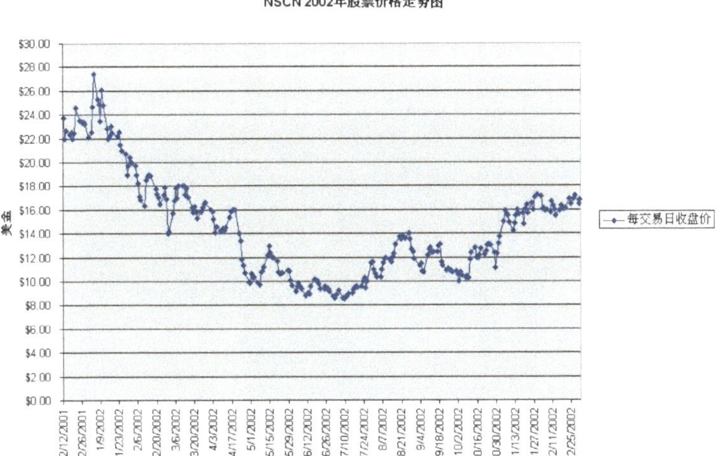

(NetScreen NSCN 2002年价格走势图)

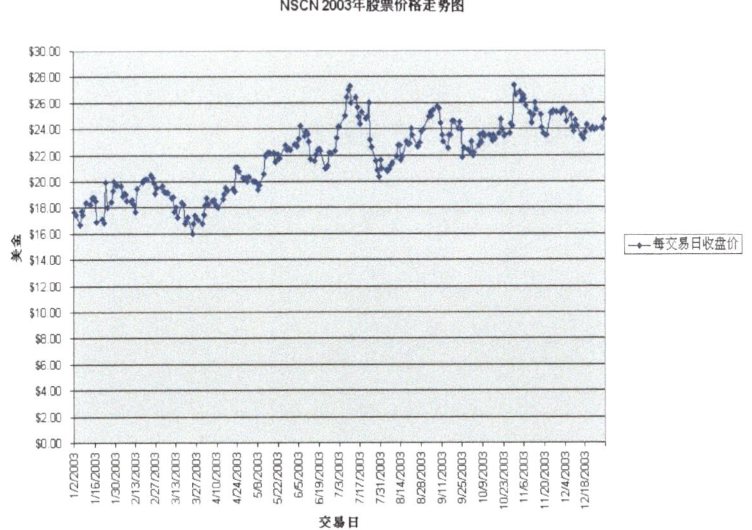

(NetScreen NSCN 2003年价格走势图)

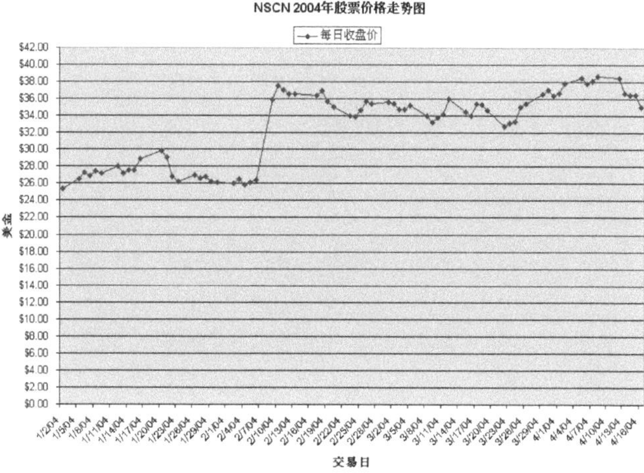

（NetScreen NSCN 2004年价格走势图）

NetScreen上市后，股价总体还是比较平稳的。在2002年的上半年，经过上市公司的锁定期后，股市持续探底，在2002年8月股价曾经跌落到8美金左右。之后，NSCN股票开始反弹并一路攀升。到2003年底的时候，公司的股价在24美金左右。市值基本上稳定在25亿美金左右。

第五章 并购之谜

NetScreen作为一个法律实体存在的6年期间，经历了被收购未遂，收购其他公司，和被Juniper Networks并购等公开的4次M&A经历。在网络安全界留下了一段令人激励和同时又很值得反思的故事。

在全球网络安全界，只要提到NetScreen，都会令人肃然起敬，被认为曾经是一个非常优秀的公司。也同时令人惋惜，觉得似乎NetScreen本可以做的更加优秀，更加成功。

2000年3月28日	Efficient Networks收购案
2002年8月22日	OneSecure收购案
2003年10月6日	Neoteris收购案
2004年2月9日	Juniper收购案

（NetScreen历次M&A案例）

下面是对NetScreen的6年期间经历的各种并购案的考察。

NetScreen与Efficient Networks的收购案

2000年3月28日，总部位于达拉斯的DSL宽带接入设备公司Efficient Networks宣布以9亿美金的股票方式收购NetScreen。下图是当时华尔街时报的相关报道：

THE WALL STREET JOURNAL.

Home World U.S. Politics Economy Business Tech Markets Opinion Arts Life Real Estate

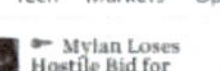

Supreme Court to Review Abortion Law in Texas · Track Federation Suspends Russian Team · Mylan Loses Hostile Bid for Perrigo · U.S. Stocks' 6-Week Win Streak Ends

TECH CENTER MAIN

Efficient Networks Plans to Acquire NetScreen for $905.9 Million in Stock

Dow Jones Newswires

Updated March 28, 2000 10:35 a.m. ET

DALLAS -- High-speed modem maker Efficient Networks Inc. agreed to acquire closely held Internet-security company NetScreen Technologies Inc. in a deal valued at $905.9 million in stock.

Efficient said it will issue 5.28 million common shares for the acquisition. Shares of Efficient closed in trading on the Nasdaq Stock Market Monday at $171.5625, up $2.5625, or 1.5%. The company currently has 53.1 million shares outstanding.

Efficient Networks said NetScreen shareholders and employees will own about 8% of the combined company.

The company named NetScreen Chief Executive Robert Thomas as president and chief operating officer of Efficient. Mr. Thomas will oversee the integration of the companies.

NetScreen has an annualized revenue run rate of $22 million and 125 employees.

Efficient said it will account for the acquisition, which it expects to complete late in its fourth quarter, as a purchase.

Efficient, of Dallas, provides DSL-based remote-access products for small and medium businesses, branch offices, telecommuters and consumers. NetScreen, of Santa Clara, Calif., offers Internet-security appliances and systems to integrate firewall, virtual private network and traffic-shaping features. Its systems are used by e-businesses, enterprises and Web-hosting and service providers.

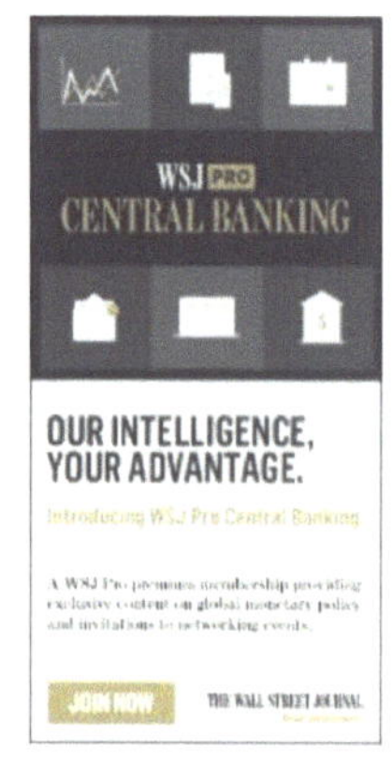

当时Efficient公司在NASDAQ的股票如日中天，当天价格为171美金。这个收购是一个纯股票收购。Efficient计划增发5百28万流通股来收购NetScreen。NetScreen如果被收购，会占Efficient公司的8%。

Efficient公司任命NetScreen的CEO Robert Thomas为Efficient的COO，全面负责这次收购和集成。

NetScreen当时有125名员工和大概2千2百万美金的营业额。

2000年4月，美国经济和股市遭遇了巨大的挫折。许多高科技公司破产，或者股票一落千丈。Efficient Networks也不幸免。在这个大环境下，2000年6月5日，Efficient Networks与NetScreen联合宣布取消3月份的收购计划。

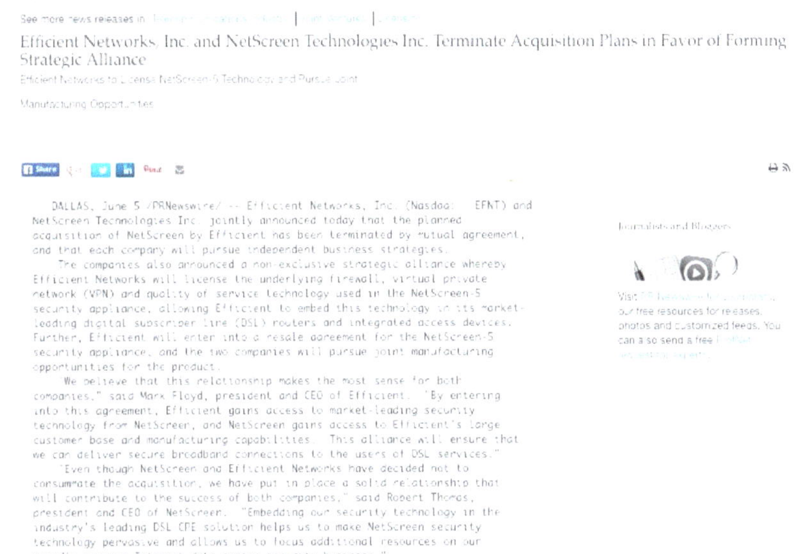

See more news releases in

Efficient Networks, Inc. and NetScreen Technologies Inc. Terminate Acquisition Plans in Favor of Forming Strategic Alliance

Efficient Networks to License NetScreen-5 Technology and Pursue Joint Manufacturing Opportunities

DALLAS, June 5 /PRNewswire/ -- Efficient Networks, Inc. (Nasdaq: EFNT) and NetScreen Technologies Inc. jointly announced today that the planned acquisition of NetScreen by Efficient has been terminated by mutual agreement, and that each company will pursue independent business strategies.

The companies also announced a non-exclusive strategic alliance whereby Efficient Networks will license the underlying firewall, virtual private network (VPN) and quality of service technology used in the NetScreen-5 security appliance, allowing Efficient to embed this technology in its market-leading digital subscriber line (DSL) routers and integrated access devices. Further, Efficient will enter into a resale agreement for the NetScreen-5 security appliance, and the two companies will pursue joint manufacturing opportunities for the product.

"We believe that this relationship makes the most sense for both companies," said Mark Floyd, president and CEO of Efficient. "By entering into this agreement, Efficient gains access to market-leading security technology from NetScreen, and NetScreen gains access to Efficient's large customer base and manufacturing capabilities. This alliance will ensure that we can deliver secure broadband connections to the users of DSL services."

"Even though NetScreen and Efficient Networks have decided not to consummate the acquisition, we have put in place a solid relationship that will contribute to the success of both companies," said Robert Thomas, president and CEO of NetScreen. "Embedding our security technology in the industry's leading DSL CPE solution helps us to make NetScreen security technology pervasive and allows us to focus additional resources on our rapidly growing Internet data center security business."

Journalists and Bloggers

Visit our free resources for releases, photos and customized feeds. You can also send a free

Efficient Networks在2000年4月股灾之后，公司一蹶不振。在不到1年后的2001年2月， Efficient Networks以15亿美金的低廉价格卖给了Siemens。

NetScreen与OneSecure的收购案

2002年8月22日，已经上市了半年的NetScreen宣布收购IPS初创公司OneSecure。价格为4千万美金。从某种意义上而言，是一个收购团队和专利的廉价收购。

NetScreen Acquires OneSecure

NEWS ANALYSIS
LIGHT READING
8/22/2002

COMMENT (1)

Login

NetScreen Technologies Inc. (Nasdaq: NSCN), a maker of carrier-class firewalls, has signed a definitive agreement to acquire intrusion prevention and detection company OneSecure Inc. (see NetScreen to Acquire OneSecure).

The deal calls for $40.3 million in NetScreen stock, with the option to use cash for some of the stock. NetScreen also will assume OneSecure's approximately $3 million in outstanding options, according to Chris Roeckl, NetScreen's director of corporate marketing.

The acquisition, which is NetScreen's first, is a significant step for the company and for the network security sector, observers say. It indicates that the market is moving towards combining firewalls with advanced intrusion detection and prevention technology.

Intrusion detection systems (IDSs) have been around for awhile and represent a growing market. In today's release, NetScreen refers to a recent report from IDC that puts the IDS market at nearly $1 billion by 2005.

Until recently though, it's proved difficult to produce IDS devices accurate enough to also perform intrusion prevention. That's because in contrast with firewalls, which *passively* control access into and out of an enterprise network based on predefined policies, IDSs *actively* scan the network looking for anomalies. This can quickly lead to data overload, as IDSs sift thousands of requests for network entry. Most vendors have focused on making IDSs more selective, instead of adding prevention, or the ability to shut down unauthorized access attempts.

"IDSs generate so much false-positive information that if they could shut down the network every time they thought there was an intrusion, they'd shut it down all the time," says Infonetics Research Inc. analyst Jeff Wilson.

收购OneSecure是NetScreen完成的第一个商业收购行为。战略思想非常正确，旨在结合防火墙Firewall与IPS的功能，并集成在一起。这个收购非常成功，直接导致了后来NetScreen产品线最重要的一个产品ISG2000+IDP插卡的问世，并获得了很不错的成功，成为NetScreen后期的旗舰产品。

OneSecure的创办人是Nir Zuk。他之前是以色列的著名网络安全公司CheckPoint的最早期的工程师之一。

Nir Zuk在OneSecure被收购之后，出任NetScreen CTO。在2006年，Nir离开已经是Juniper网络安全事业部的NetScreen，创办PaloAlto Networks公司。其主要技术路线其实就是把当年OneSecure做的IPS工作与Firewall做深度的耦合，提出了Application ID的概念，并在工业界力推NGFW(Next Generation Firewall)的产品方向。PaloAlto Networks在2012年7月20日成功

在NASDAQ上市并获得了巨大的成功。PaloAlto Networks的市值目前为140亿美金左右，成为全球网络安全领域，特别是NGFW领头的公司之一。

NetScreen与Neoteris的收购案

2003年10月6日， NetScreen宣布收购SSL/VPN公司Neoteris。收购价格为2.45亿美金的股票交换和2千万现金。 如果Neoteris在未来的一个时间段营收达到一个目标值，NetScreen会另外给Neoteris的股票拥有者3千万美金。

Neoteris是公认的在SSL/VPN方面的领头公司。当时全球已经有近600个客户。 其CEO是Krishna "Kittu" Kolluri。Juniper收购NetScreen之后， Kittu后来成为Juniper网络安全事业部的负责人负责人。

由于NetScreen公司自己在2004年初被Juniper公司收购。导致NetScreen对Neoteris的收购和集成基本上没有完成，最后导致是与NetScreen被收购同时完成的并入Juniper。

一个很令人深思的事情是， 当NetScreen被收购后，NetScreen的管理团队基本上在一年内都离开了Juniper，反而是Neoteris的管理团队基本上接管了之前的NetScreen。

NetScreen To Acquire Neoteris, SSL VPN Market Leader

Accelerates NetScreen's Strategy to Drive Application-level Security into the Network Infrastructure

Monday, October 6, 2003 5:06 am PDT

Dateline:

SUNNYVALE, Calif.

Public Company Information:

NASDAQ:JNPR

NetScreen Technologies, Inc. (Nasdaq: NSCN) today announced that it has signed a definitive agreement to acquire Neoteris®, Inc., the market leader in the SSL virtual private network (VPN) product category as well as a leader in the application security gateway market, for approximately $245 million in stock and $20 million in cash at the closing, including assumption of all outstanding Neoteris options. Upon the achievement of certain revenue milestones, NetScreen will pay Neoteris stockholders and optionholders up to an additional $30 million in cash.

"Our clientless SSL solution has been well received and adopted by many highly recognized enterprise customers"

（NetScreen收购Neoteris的新闻）

NetScreen与Juniper的并购

2004年2月9日,全球第二大网络通讯设备公司 Juniper Networks. 以NetScreen 股票NSCN 2月6日市值26.40美金为基点,出价约40亿美金并购NetScreen。每股NetScreen的流通股(NASDAQ：NSCN)换成1.404的Juniper的流通股(NASDAQ：JNPR)。NetScreen股票持有人共占Juniper股票的24.5%.

当时，NetScreen的市值为24亿美金。 2003年可统计的营业额是2.75亿美金。 Juniper相当于在NetScreen市值24亿美金的价格上，付了67%左右的额外佣金，**Juniper为了收购NetScreen整体付出的价格是NetScreen 2003年营收的15倍**。

华尔街对Juniper出这个价格的反应有不少疑虑。其中最突出的是华尔街时报的一篇分析文章认为，这是Juniper董事会为了满足当时的CEO Scott 2004年的奖金KPI而特意做的局。是一种洗钱行为。

TECH

The 'I Must Do a Merger' Bonus

By
SCOTT THURM Staff Reporter of THE WALL STREET JOURNAL
Updated April 6, 2004 12:01 a.m. ET

Want a bonus? Acquire a company.

That's the unusual deal that directors of Juniper Networks Inc. gave to Chief Executive Scott Kriens. According to filings with the Securities and Exchange Commission, Mr. Kriens's bonus for this year is dependent on Juniper's "entry into new businesses by means of acquisitions." The board is serious: Without an acquisition, no Juniper executive will get a bonus, according to the filings.

They don't need to worry. On Feb. 9, Juniper, a Sunnyvale, Calif., maker of Internet-switching gear, said it plans to acquire security-technology specialist Netscreen Technologies Inc., also of Sunnyvale,

当然，Juniper否认了这一点。但可以相信的是，在这个高价格的诱惑下，NetScreen的董事会和管理团队的大多数人是投了赞成票。毕竟董事会只是资本的代言人。而资本的本质是要安全获利，而非赌未来是否存在一个百亿美金市值的安全企业。

Juniper Networks, Inc. to Acquire NetScreen Technologies, Inc.

Combination provides comprehensive, best in class networking solutions

Monday, February 9, 2004 5:08 am PST

Dateline:

SUNNYVALE, Calif.

Public Company Information:

NASDAQ:JNPR

Juniper Networks, Inc. (Nasdaq: JNPR) has signed an agreement to acquire NetScreen Technologies, Inc. (Nasdaq: NSCN), in a stock for stock merger transaction. Based upon Juniper Networks closing stock price of $29.47 on February 6, 2004, the deal has an approximate value of $4 billion. Juniper Networks stock will be exchanged for NetScreen Technologies stock at a fixed exchange ratio of 1.404 shares of Juniper Networks common stock for each outstanding share of NetScreen Technologies common stock. The combined company will provide customers with mission critical networking requirements, including security, reliability and performance, each simultaneously without compromise.

"Our collective customers have told us security, reliability and performance are mission critical to their network users, and together we will deliver a compelling response to their needs."

（Juniper收购NetScreen的正式通告）

NetScreen与Juniper的收购在2004年的4月16日完成。4月19日，NetScreen的股票在NASDAQ正式停牌。

Juniper Networks Completes Acquisition of NetScreen Technologies and Appoints Frank J. Marshall to the Juniper Networks Board of Directors

Friday, April 16, 2004 5:08 am PDT

Dateline:

SUNNYVALE, Calif.

Public Company Information:

NASDAQ:JNPR

Juniper Networks, Inc. (Nasdaq: JNPR) today announced that it has completed its acquisition of NetScreen Technologies, Inc. The trading of NetScreen common stock (Nasdaq: NSCN) will be suspended before the opening of the market on April 19, 2004.

"We're pleased to welcome Frank to the Juniper Networks board"

Juniper Networks also announced that, under the terms of the transaction requiring the appointment of a designee of NetScreen to the board of directors, Frank J. Marshall has been appointed to the Juniper Networks board of directors as a Class III director with a term expiring in 2005. Mr. Marshall will be replacing Vinod Khosla, who has been a significant contributor to the board of directors since 1996.

(Juniper完成对NetScreen的收购)

NetScreen在收购Neoteris之后，在还没有进行集成和整合，就立刻被Juniper收购的过程(相距4个月，其中含有感恩节和圣诞节假期)。基本上可以说明Juniper对NetScreen的收购是一个来自Juniper董事会的行为，而非NetScreen的主动求卖。NetScreen董事会在高溢价的并购协议前，选择了退出。

资本退出无可厚非。资本的目的就是赚钱，而非做一个伟大的企业。但是NetScreen的董事会没有妥善的处理Neoteris收购后的集成和人事安排问题，为NetScreen并入Juniper后的各个方面都带来了一些遗留问题，例如，当NetScreen的管理团队离开之后，NetScreen的华人研发队伍基本上失去了对未来的控制。

第六章 十年得失

站在2016年的今天，回头看当年网络安全界的这个影响力至今犹存的并购，基本上公认这是一次令人惋惜的战略举措。NetScreen当年日新月异的研发和扩张被消磨严重。各种财务数据表明Juniper安全产品的营业额已经是连续6年的负增长。

站在客观的角度， 当年邓锋和柯严作为创办人即使从个人对自己创办的公司有感情的角度，不愿意卖公司，也可能没有办法逆转。他们当时是研发副总裁和首席架构师，而且邓锋在董事会里只有一个席位，即使投反对票，也无法逆转。另外，从资本的角度，Juniper当时的确给出了在当时一个令NetScreen董事会很难拒绝的价格。

从Juniper收购NetScreen之后的10年的发展来看，华尔街和工业界基本上都一致同意：Juniper与NetScreen是一次错误的结合。耽误了NetScreen的发展，否则NetScreen完全可能成长为一个百亿美金的世界级的科技大公司。

并购是在2004年的4月完成。完成后，Juniper的领导层成员如下图所示。我们可以发现，前NetScreen的管理层基本上全部出局。只有前NetScreen收购的Neoteris公司的CEO Kittu进入了Juniper管理层。NetScreen早期的管理团队和创办人邓锋和柯严都出局，或者是在双方默认的有条件的逐步退出了。

NAME	AGE	POSITION
Scott Kriens	47	Chief Executive Officer and Chairman of the Board
Pradeep Sindhu	52	Chief Technical Officer and Vice Chairman of the Board
James A. Dolce Jr.	42	Executive Vice President, Field Operations
Robert R.B. Dykes	55	Executive Vice President, Business Operations and Chief Financial Officer*
Marcel Gani	52	Executive Vice President, Chief Financial Officer
Krishna "Kittu" Kolluri	41	Executive Vice President and General Manager of the Security Products Group
Carol Mills	51	Executive Vice President and General Manager of the Infrastructure Products Group

（Juniper于2004年的管理团队）

Juniper为NetScreen的收购付出的代价总共是41亿美金。其41亿美金的各个细节为：

Net tangible assets (liabilities) assumed	$ 373.9
Amortizable intangible assets:	
Existing technology	165.2
Maintenance agreements	5.9
Patents and core technology	45.7
Trade name and trademarks	8.3
Value-added reseller relationships	14.7
Distributor relationships	10.1
Order backlog	2.5
Total amortizable intangible assets	252.4
In-process research and development	27.5
Deferred compensation on unvested stock options	93.5
Goodwill	3,437.8
Total purchase price	$4,185.1

其中专利和核心技术估值4千5百7十万美金。值得注意的是NetScreen的渠道和分销商的关系被折算为2千4百8十万美金。Juniper对NetScreen的并购为Juniper带来了两个价值：运营商级别的网络安全产品和企业网市场的网络安全产品，同时NetScreen在企业网市场积累的销售渠道也为Juniper的路由器产品（例如，M Series）在企业网的销售打开了窗户。

同时，Juniper在运营商市场的巨大积累也为NetScren的安全产品销售进入运营商市场提供了巨大的机会。

收购NetScreen之后，Juniper具备了强大的企业网的入口，并整合形成了两大主力产品线(Infrastructure和Service Layer Technologies)，并且形成交叉销售。其中，SLT主要是以NetScreen的安全产品线为主，但也包括了一些收购的小公司，例如，Funk，Peribit，Redline，Kagoor等。

Juniper收购NetScreen之后，运营商解决方案获得了加强，企业解决方案得到了从0到1的增强。营收不断提高。在2010年，Juniper的网络安全产品线的营收达到了其历史的最高峰，高达7.47亿美金。成为Juniper整个公司里最重要的产品线和解决方案之一。但之后开始持续回落。

下面是对NetScreen产品线并入Juniper之后的2004年到2014年营收变化的一个详细分析。

NetScreen产品线2004年营收：

在Juniper于2005年3月发布的关于2004年的年报里可以发现，NetScreen安全产品线的2004年的营收为1亿8千7百万美金(注：应该是2004年4月19日之后的合并报表）。是Juniper在2014年总营收的16.1%。如果算上NetScreen财政年从2003年10月1日到2004年9月30日，NetScreen的产品销售额大概为3亿美金。

NetScreen产品线2005年营收：

2005年的年度财报里，Juniper的网络安全产品线的营收是4.03亿美金，占Juniper总体产品销售（Product Sales）营收的23%。Juniper高度评价了安全产品在企业网市场的增长。“Our higher net revenues in 2005 as compared to 2004 primarily due to the revenue growth from Security products. Additionally, the acquisitions made in 2005 enabled us to cross sell infrastructure, security, and application acceleration products to existing customer bases.”

	Year Ended December 31,		
	2005	2004	2003
Net Revenues:			
Infrastructure	$ 1,367.8	$ 975.7	$ 602.5
Service Layer Technologies	403.2	187.2	—
Service	293.0	173.1	98.9
Total net revenues	$ 2,064.0	$ 1,336.0	$ 701.4
Operating Income:			
Management operating income:			
Infrastructure	$ 483.2	$ 297.9	$ 76.1
Service Layer Technologies	13.4	1.0	—
Service	72.3	32.6	17.6
Total management operating income	568.9	331.5	93.7
Amortization of purchased intangible assets	(85.2)	(56.8)	(20.7)
Stock-based compensation expense related to acquisitions	(17.6)	(44.0)	(2.0)
IPR&D	(11.0)	(27.5)	—
Restructuring, impairments, and special charges, net	0.6	5.1	(14.0)
Patent expense	(10.0)	—	—
Integration costs	—	(5.1)	—
Total operating income	$ 445.7	$ 203.2	$ 57.0

在2005年的4.03亿美金里，其中3.99亿美金属于产品销售。在后面的几年，Juniper通过两个产品线的配合，在过去已经存在的客户群里做交叉和后续销售。

2006年开始，Juniper在重组之后，NetScreen产品线以Juniper SLT事业群的方式展开研发和销售。

NetScreen产品线2006年营收：

2006年， SLT的产品销售额为4.79亿美金。比2005年增长20%，占Juniper公司的总营收的25%。需要注意的是4.79亿美金里虽然主要是安全产品，但也包括一些2005年收购的一些小公司带来的营收，例如，Kagoor， Redline， Peribit等等。但这些小公司的产品营收都比较小。

	Year Ended December 31,		
	2006	2005 As Restated (1)	2004 As Restated (1)
Net Revenues:			
Infrastructure	$ 1,413.4	$ 1,371.6	$ 975.7
Service Layer Technologies	479.9	399.4	187.2
Service	410.3	293.0	173.1
Total net revenues	2,303.6	2,064.0	1,336.0
Operating Income:			
Management operating income:			
Infrastructure	420.0	487.4	304.4
Service Layer Technologies	(12.8)	9.6	(5.5)
Service	101.3	71.9	32.6
Total management operating income	508.5	568.9	331.5
Amortization of purchased intangible assets (2)	(97.3)	(85.2)	(56.8)
Stock-based compensation expense	(87.6)	(22.3)	(54.9)
Impairment of goodwill and intangible assets	(1,283.4)	(5.9)	—
In-process research and development	—	(11.0)	(27.5)
Other expense, net (3)	(38.0)	(3.5)	—
Total operating (loss) income	(997.8)	441.0	192.3
Interest and other income	104.3	59.1	28.2
Interest and other expense	(3.6)	(3.9)	(5.4)
Gain on (write-down of) investment, net	—	1.3	(2.9)
Loss on redemption of convertible subordinated notes	—	—	(4.1)
(Loss) income before income taxes	$ (897.1)	$ 497.5	$ 208.1

NetScreen产品线2007年营收：

2007年，SLT的5.74亿美金。占总收入的20%。增长主要得益于企业网对安全产品的需求，和与运营商市场的交叉销售。

	Years Ended December 31,				Years Ended December 31,			
	2007	2006	$ Change	% Change	2006	2005	$ Change	% Change
Net revenues:								
Infrastructure	$1,753.2	$ 1,413.4	$ 339.8	24%	$ 1,413.4	$1,371.6	$ 41.8	3%
Service Layer Technologies	573.8	479.9	93.9	20%	479.9	399.4	80.5	20%
Service	509.1	410.3	98.8	24%	410.3	293.0	117.3	40%
Total net revenues	$2,836.1	$ 2,303.6	$ 532.5	23%	$ 2,303.6	$2,064.0	$ 239.6	12%

NetScreen产品线2008年营收分析：

2008年，SLT的营收为6亿美金。增长主要得益于企业网对安全产品的需求，和与运营商市场的交叉销售。但增长的速度相对2007年在放缓，只有6%的增长。

	Years Ended December 31,				Years Ended December 31,			
	2008	2007(1)	$ Change	% Change	2007(1)	2006(1)	$ Change	% Change
Net revenues:								
Infrastructure:								
Product	$2,301.9	$1,753.2	$ 548.7	31%	$1,753.2	$ 1,413.4	$ 339.8	24%
Service	424.0	320.1	103.9	32%	320.1	266.7	53.4	20%
Total Infrastructure revenues	2,725.9	2,073.3	652.6	31%	2,073.3	1,680.1	393.2	23%
Service Layer Technologies:								
Product	609.1	573.8	35.3	6%	573.8	479.9	93.9	20%
Service	237.4	189.0	48.4	26%	189.0	143.6	45.4	32%
Total Service Layer Technologies revenues	846.5	762.8	83.7	11%	762.8	623.5	139.3	22%
Total net revenues	3,572.4	2,836.1	736.3	26%	2,836.1	2,303.6	532.5	23%

NetScreen产品线2009年营收：

2009年，SLT的产品销售收入出现不增长的现象，维持在6亿美金的水平，比2008年略微降低。

	Years Ended December 31,				Years Ended December 31,			
	2009	2008	$ Change	% Change	2008	2007	$ Change	% Change
Net revenues:								
Infrastructure:								
Product	$1,959.2	$2,301.9	$ (342.7)	(15)%	$2,301.9	$1,753.2	$ 548.7	31%
Service	482.4	424.0	58.4	14%	424.0	320.1	103.9	32%
Total Infrastructure revenues	2,441.6	2,725.9	(284.3)	(10)%	2,725.9	2,073.3	652.6	31%
Service Layer Technologies:								
Product	608.8	609.1	(0.3)	N/M	609.1	573.8	35.3	6%
Service	265.5	237.4	28.1	12%	237.4	189.0	48.4	26%
Total Service Layer Technologies revenues	874.3	846.5	27.8	3%	846.5	762.8	83.7	11%
Total net revenues	3,315.9	3,572.4	(256.5)	(7)%	3,572.4	2,836.1	736.3	26%

NetScreen产品线2010年营收：

2010年，SLT由于SRX产品线的成功，特别是高端系统SRX5800的成功，和美国经济的复苏，产品销售增长很快，产品销售额达到历史的最高点7.47亿美金。

如果加上服务营收（Service Revenue）的2亿9千5百万美金，SLT产品线第一次突破10亿美金，为10亿4千3百万美金。占Juniper年总收入的25%左右。

	Years Ended December 31,				Years Ended December 31,			
	2010	2009	$ Change	% Change	2009	2008	$ Change	% Change
Net revenues:								
Infrastructure:								
Product	$ 2,511.6	$ 1,959.2	$ 552.4	28%	$ 1,959.2	$ 2,301.9	$ (342.7)	(15)%
Service	538.7	482.4	56.3	12%	482.4	424.0	58.4	14 %
Total Infrastructure revenues	3,050.3	2,441.6	608.7	25%	2,441.6	2,725.9	(284.3)	(10)%
SLT:								
Product	747.1	608.8	138.3	23%	608.8	609.1	(0.3)	N/M
Service	295.9	265.5	30.4	11%	265.5	237.4	28.1	12 %
Total SLT revenues	1,043.0	874.3	168.7	19%	874.3	846.5	27.8	3 %
Total net revenues	4,093.3	3,315.9	777.4	23%	3,315.9	3,572.4	(256.5)	(7)%

NetScreen产品线2011年营收：

2011年， SLT的产品销售开始放缓， 比2010年回落了7%，为6.97亿美金。加上服务营收， SLT还维持在10亿美金的范围。Juniper在年度报表中认为SLT营收的回落主要是由于SRX产品在运营商里布网的延缓和老客户往SRX产品过渡的周期问题。

“SLT product revenue also had a slight decrease in 2011, compared to 2010, primarily attributed to the decline in our high-end product lines influenced by the timing of our high-end SRX service provider deployments and the transition from older enterprise security products to our new security product portfolio. ”

SLT

	Years Ended December 31,				Years Ended December 31,			
	2011	2010	$ Change	% Change	2010	2009	$ Change	% Change
	(in millions, except percentages and units)							
SLT segment revenues:								
SLT product revenue	$ 697.7	$ 747.1	$ (49.4)	(7)%	$ 747.1	$ 608.8	$ 138.3	23%
Percentage of net revenues	*15.7 %*	*18.3 %*			*18.3 %*	*18.4 %*		
SLT service revenue	328.4	295.9	32.5	11%	295.9	265.5	30.4	11%
Percentage of net revenues	*7.4 %*	*7.2 %*			*7.2 %*	*8.0 %*		
Total SLT segment revenues	$ 1,026.1	$ 1,043.0	$ (16.9)	(2)%	$ 1,043.0	$ 874.3	$ 168.7	19%
Percentage of net revenues	*23.1 %*	*25.5 %*			*25.5 %*	*26.4 %*		
SLT revenue units	252,848	231,365	21,483	9%	231,365	208,907	22,458	11%
SLT operating income (1)	$ 199.0	$ 208.0	$ (9.0)	(4)%	$ 208.0	$ 127.0	$ 81.0	64%
Percentage of SLT revenues	*19.4 %*	*19.9 %*			*19.9 %*	*14.5 %*		

(1) A reconciliation of total segment operating income to income before taxes and noncontrolling interest can be found in Note 13, *Segments*, in Notes to Consolidated Financial Statement in Item 8 of this Form 10-K.

NetScreen产品线2012年营收：

2012年Juniper开始在财务和组织结构上把产品划分为PSD(Platform Systems Division)和SSD(Software Solution Division)两大组织，在财报里不再使用Infrastructure和SLT的架构。

“Beginning in the first quarter of 2012, we aligned our organizational structure to focus on our platform and software strategy, which resulted in two reportable segments organized principally by product families: Platform Systems Division ("PSD") and Software Solutions Division ("SSD"). Our PSD segment primarily offers scalable routing and switching products that are used in service provider, enterprise, and public sector networks to control and direct network traffic between data centers, core, edge, aggregation, campus, Wide Area Networks ("WANs"), branch, and consumer and business devices. Our SSD segment offers software solutions focused on network security and network services applications for both service providers and enterprise customers. Together, our high-performance product and service offerings help our customers to convert legacy networks that provide commoditized services into more valuable assets that provide differentiation, value, and increased performance, reliability, and security to end-users. ”

Software Solutions Division Segment
(in millions, except percentages)

	Years Ended December 31,						
	2012	2011	2010	2012 vs. 2011		2011 vs. 2010	
				$ Change	% Change	$ Change	% Change
SSD product revenues:							
Security/Other	$ 493.3	$ 490.6	$ 539.4	$ 2.7	1%	$ (48.8)	(9)%
Routing	84.7	112.7	95.8	(28.0)	(25)%	16.9	18%
Total SSD product revenues	578.0	603.3	635.2	(25.3)	(4)%	(31.9)	(5)%
SSD service revenues	269.0	257.1	231.3	11.9	5%	25.8	11%
Total SSD revenues	$ 847.0	$ 860.4	$ 866.5	$ (13.4)	(2)%	$ (6.1)	(1)%
SSD contribution margin (*)	$ 340.6	$ 345.0	$ 405.0	$ (4.4)	(1)%	$ (60.0)	(15)%
Percentage of SSD revenues	*40.2 %*	*40.1 %*	*46.7 %*				

(*) A reconciliation of contribution margin to income before taxes and noncontrolling interest can be found in Note 13, *Segments*, in Notes to Consolidated Financial Statement in Item 8 of this Report.

Platform Systems Division Segment
(in millions, except percentages)

	Years Ended December 31,						
	2012	2011	2010	2012 vs. 2011		2011 vs. 2010	
				$ Change	% Change	$ Change	% Change
PSD product revenues:							
Routing	$ 1,946.8	$ 2,166.0	$ 2,034.7	$ (219.2)	(10)%	$ 131.3	6%
Switching	554.8	495.8	377.7	59.0	12%	118.1	31%
Security/Other	182.5	213.2	211.1	(30.7)	(14)%	2.1	1%
Total PSD product revenues	2,684.1	2,875.0	2,623.5	(190.9)	(7)%	251.5	10%
PSD service revenues	834.3	713.3	603.3	121.0	17%	110.0	18%
Total PSD revenues	$ 3,518.4	$ 3,588.3	$ 3,226.8	$ (69.9)	(2)%	$ 361.5	11%
PSD contribution margin (*)	$ 1,409.4	$ 1,586.2	$ 1,477.9	$ (176.8)	(11)%	$ 108.3	7%
Percentage of PSD revenues	*40.1 %*	*44.2 %*	*45.8 %*				

之前在SLT里的网络安全产品线，例如，NetScreen被收购后产生的SRX产品线按照应用场景被划分在PSD和SSD中(主要是计算在SSD中)。因此，在财务上，安全产品，特别是SRX产品，有一些是在PSD中。之前NetScreen的产品，例如ISG防火墙系列，都归属在SSD中。

从上述2012年度财报可以看到，安全产品线的产品销售为6.69亿美金，比2011年再次下跌4%。从财报分析来看，其主要原因是高中档防火墙的销售不好。

"*2012 Compared to 2011*

SSD product revenues decreased in 2012, compared to 2011, primarily due to a decline in the sales of our high-end and branch firewall products and routing services products, partially offset by an increase in sales of our high-end SRX products. SSD service revenues increased in 2012, compared to 2011, primarily driven by strong contract renewals for support services.”

这是自2010年以后的连续两年安全产品线的产品销售额跌落。

NetScreen产品线2013年营收：

2013年，Juniper调整了企业网产品线，特别是网络安全产品线。所有的安全产品都归属于SSD。有点类似之前的Infrastructure/SLT架构。

2013年，SSD产品销售持续下滑为5.64亿美金。在财报中Juniper认为主要原因是安全产品的销售下降是整个SSD业绩不好的主要原因，特别是高端SRX产品在运营商领域的销售不好。

“SSD product revenues decreased in 2013, compared to 2012, primarily due to a decline in sales of security products, driven by lower demand for high-end SRX products by service providers. Revenues from branch SRX security products improved slightly in 2013, compared to 2012. SSD service revenues increased in 2013, compared to 2012, primarily driven by strong contract renewals for support services.”

Software Solutions Division Segment
(in millions, except percentages)

	Years Ended December 31,						
	2013	2012	2011	2013 vs. 2012		2012 vs. 2011	
				$ Change	% Change	$ Change	% Change
SSD product revenues:							
Security	$ 564.3	$ 669.9	$ 698.3	$ (105.6)	(16)%	$ (28.4)	(4)%
Routing	74.0	90.6	118.1	(16.6)	(18)%	(27.5)	(23)%
Total SSD product revenues	638.3	760.5	816.4	(122.2)	(16)%	(55.9)	(7)%
SSD service revenues	352.6	334.1	325.4	18.5	6%	8.7	3%
Total SSD revenues	$ 990.9	$ 1,094.6	$ 1,141.8	$ (103.7)	(9)%	$ (47.2)	(4)%
SSD contribution margin (*)	$ 398.4	$ 473.6	$ 504.4	$ (75.2)	(16)%	$ (30.8)	(6)%
Percentage of SSD revenues	*40.2 %*	*43.3 %*	*44.2 %*				

(*) A reconciliation of contribution margin to income before income taxes and noncontrolling interest can be found in Note 13, *Segments*, in Notes to Consolidated Financial Statement in Item 8 of this Report.

NetScreen产品线2014年营收：

2014年，Juniper再次调整，取消了PSD和SSD的划分。整个公司在财务上不再区分运营商和企业网的区别。在营业额方面，各个方面都还在下滑，包括路由产品(Routing)，交换产品

(Switching)和安全(Security)。其中，安全产品的销售额只为4.63亿美金。

	Years Ended December 31,						
	2014	2013	2012	2014 vs. 2013		2013 vs. 2012	
				$ Change	% Change	$ Change	% Change
Routing	$ 2,223.9	$ 2,318.0	$ 2,037.6	$ (94.1)	(4)%	$ 280.4	14%
Switching	721.2	638.0	554.8	83.2	13 %	83.2	15%
Security	463.6	563.9	669.7	(100.3)	(18)%	(105.8)	(16)%
Total Product	3,408.7	3,519.9	3,262.1	(111.2)	(3)%	257.8	8%
Percentage of net revenues	*73.7 %*	*75.4 %*	*74.7 %*				
Total Service	1,218.4	1,149.2	1,103.3	69.2	6 %	45.9	4%
Percentage of net revenues	*26.3 %*	*24.6 %*	*25.3 %*				
Total net revenues	$ 4,627.1	$ 4,669.1	$ 4,365.4	$ (42.0)	(1)%	$ 303.7	7%

2014 Compared to 2013

Juniper在年度财报中表示，安全产品持续下滑的原因是因为之前的NetScreen ScreenOS产品的持续下滑(例如，ISG2000)和SRX产品线的不增长。

“Security product net revenues decreased in 2014, compared to 2013, primarily due to a continuing decline in our legacy Screen OS products and the divestiture of our Junos Pulse product lines. Sales of our SRX platform declined slightly year-over-year, due to lower demand from U.S. Carrier customers. ”

NetScreen产品线2015年营收：

2015年，Juniper在营业额方面，路由产品线和交换机产品线的业绩有所回升，但安全产品线的业绩还是在持续下降，总共只有435.6M美金的收入，比2014年的安全产品线收入再次减少了6%。形势很不乐观。

	Years Ended December 31,				
	2015	2014	2013	2015 vs. 2014	
				$ Change	% Change
Routing	$ 2,359.2	$ 2,223.9	$ 2,318.0	$ 135.3	6 %
Switching	768.3	721.2	638.0	47.1	7 %
Security	435.6	463.6	563.9	(28.0)	(6)%
Total Product	3,563.1	3,408.7	3,519.9	154.4	5 %
Percentage of net revenues	*73.3%*	*73.7%*	*75.4%*		
Total Service	1,294.7	1,218.4	1,149.2	76.3	6 %
Percentage of net revenues	*26.7%*	*26.3%*	*24.6%*		
Total net revenues	$ 4,857.8	$ 4,627.1	$ 4,669.1	$ 230.7	5 %

安全产品线已经是连续6年的下滑。 Juniper的年报是这样解释其原因的：“Security product net revenues decreased in 2015, compared to 2014, primarily due to the divestiture of our Junos Pulse product lines and a continuing decline in our ScreenOS products, which was partially offset by an increase in sales of our SRX platform and security software year-over-year. Additionally, we also saw a decrease in security net revenues within the enterprise market, which was partially offset by a slight increase in the service provider market.”

可以看出，在企业网市场，Juniper的NetScreen和延伸的SRX产品线还是在持续丢失市场份额。

下面是NetScreen/Juniper在1998年--2004年的6年里，安全产品销售的数字如下(单位：百万美金)：

1998年	0.648
1999年	5.66
2000年	23.4
2001年	71.2
2002年	113.9
2003年	200.4
2004年	300

我们可以发现，NetScreen产品一直在非常大幅度的占领市场份额，特别是在上市之后的2003和2004年。

下面是NetScreen／Juniper在2004年--2015年的12年里，安全产品销售的数字如下(单位：百万美金)：

2005年	399.4
2006年	479.9
2007年	573.8
2008年	609.1
2009年	608.8
2010年	747.1
2011年	698.3
2012年	669.9
2013年	564.3
2014年	463.6
2015年	435.6

我们可以很容易的发现，NetScreen并入Juniper，合并报表后，Juniper在企业网，特别是网络安全方面的营收持续增加，特别是在2010年，达到了顶峰，高达7亿4千7百万美金。然后，就持续下滑。截至目前为止，已经是连续6年的负增长。

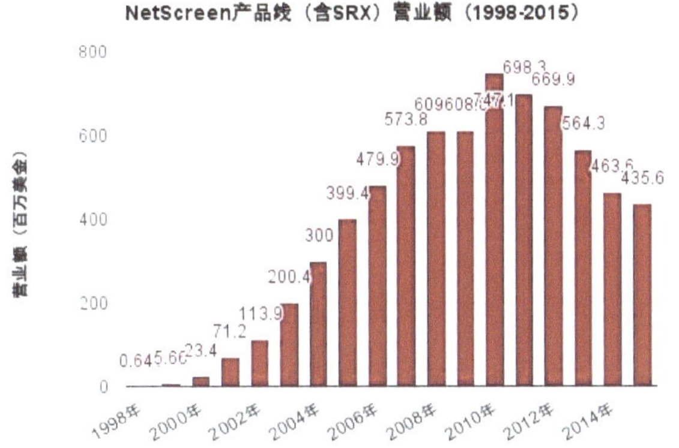

（NetScreen产品线1998-2015年历年营业额）

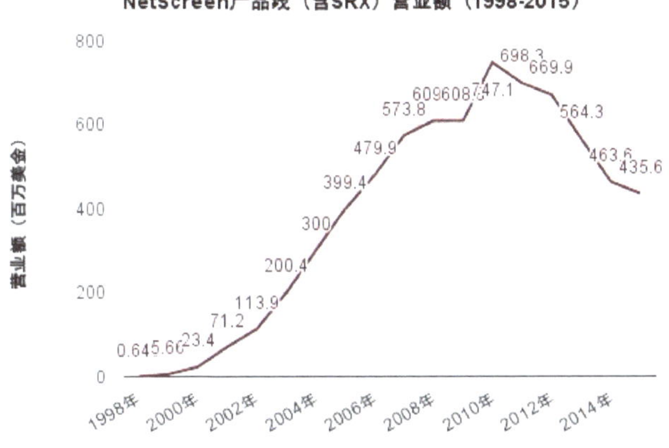

（NetScreen产品线1998-2015年历年营业额）

Gartner是业界著名的智库和战略咨询公司，是工业界公认的对产业发展，科技公司所处的位置的重要话语权机构之一，特别是其对各个产品的魔力象限矩阵画像，影响力非常大，是许多产品采购公司的重要考虑因素之一。

下面图示是Gartner从2008到2015年的企业防火墙的评估魔力象限图。

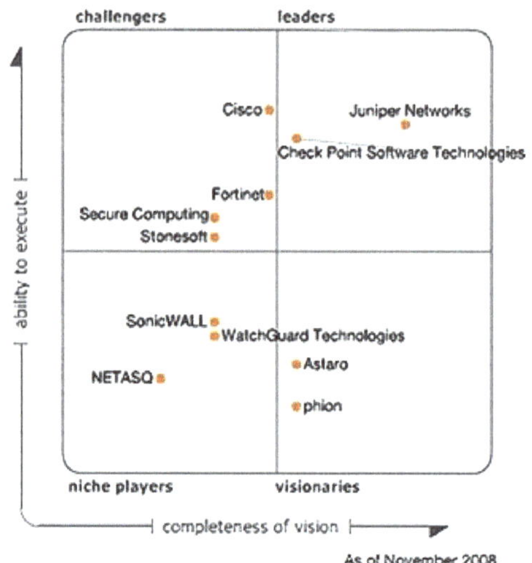

(Gartner 2008年企业防火墙象限)

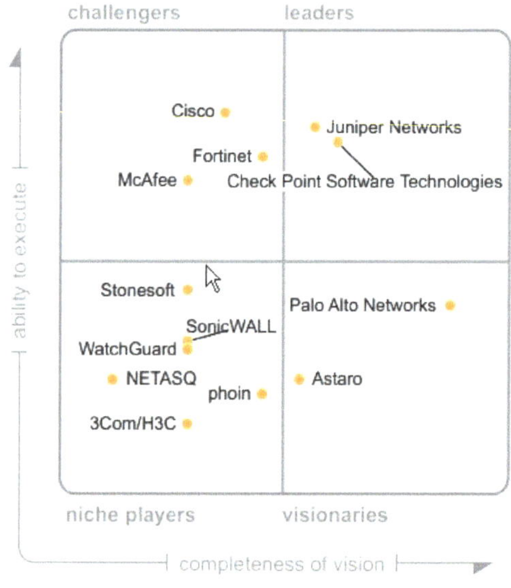

(Gartner 2010年企业防火墙象限)

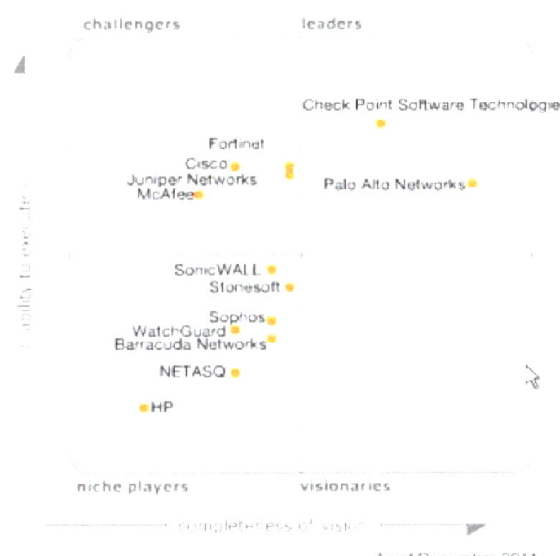

(Gartner 2011年企业防火墙象限)

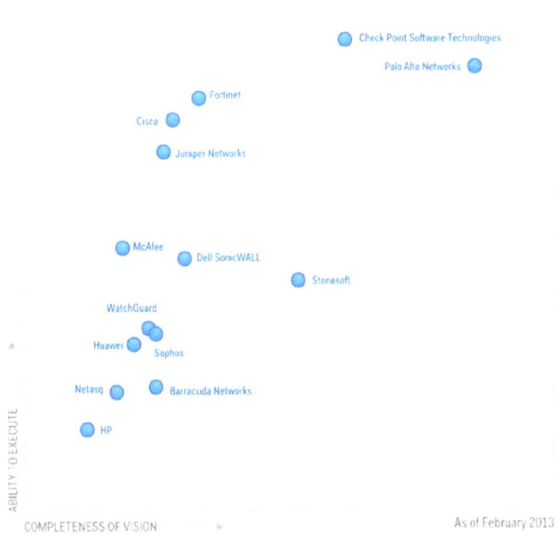

(Gartner 2013年企业防火墙象限)

(Gartner 2014年企业防火墙象限)

(Gartner 2015年企业防火墙象限)

研究Gartner历年关于企业防火墙的魔力象限数据的演变，我们可以很容易的发现：

NetScreen和Juniper安全产品线在2008，2009，2010年一直都处于业界领先地位，在企业安全防火墙领域，稳定的在第一象限，处于领导者的地位（市场份额和创新能力）。但从2011年，开始第一次跌出第一象限。然后在最近的几年持续的丢失市场份额，**在2015年，已经跌落到第4象限。**在创新能力方面，值得注意的是，从NetScreen和Juniper的安全产品线出来的山石网络已经在2014年，2015年成功进入Gartner的企业防火墙象限，并在创新能力方面表现的很亮眼。

NetScreen并购案十年的反思：

NetScreen在研发，市场都在最高峰的时候，被Juniper高溢价收购，使得NetScreen的独立发展乍然而止，让网络和安全界，让硅谷华人社区，都觉得惋惜。

如果Juniper并购NetScreen之后，NetScreen产品线能够在一个更大的市场空间得以发展壮大，也不失为一个好的结合。但过去的十年，事实是一个令人扼腕的故事，通过收购NetScreen形成的Juniper的网络安全产品线不断丢失市场份额，流失研发骨干人才。从某种意义上而言，已经是大势已去。

2014年1月，华尔街著名的对冲基金Elliott Management发布了一个很有影响力的调查报告--"Juniper Networks--Elliott Management's Perspectives"。调查报告对Juniper过去10年公司业绩一直低迷做出了详尽的分析，并提出了重要的改革建议。其中，对Juniper收购NetScreen之后的错误重组提出了批评。

例如，在描述Juniper错过的机遇窗口时，Elliott Management如此说到："Pure-play security vendors today have a combined market cap of ~$30B. NetScreen was a leader and would have been more valuable and successful had it not lost share under Juniper's ownership"。

其意思是：业界安全厂商的市值总共已经有了300亿美金。NetScreen作为当年网络安全市场的领导者，如果不是在Juniper的旗下，本可以变的更加有价值和更加成功。从2003年到2012年， 安全设备市场一直在以20%的CAGR成长。然而Juniper在网络安全的市场份额从2003年的14%，跌落到2013年的6%的份额。

Elliott Management's Perspectives

January 13, 2014

（华尔街著名对冲基金Elliott Management的调查报告）

由于Juniper对企业市场缺乏基因，并且对并购企业（M&A）的缺乏经验，导致在浪费了巨多的现金流之后，还错失了重要的机遇。许多金融分析师建议应该从新考虑Juniper在安全产品线的战略，包括把安全产品线剥离。

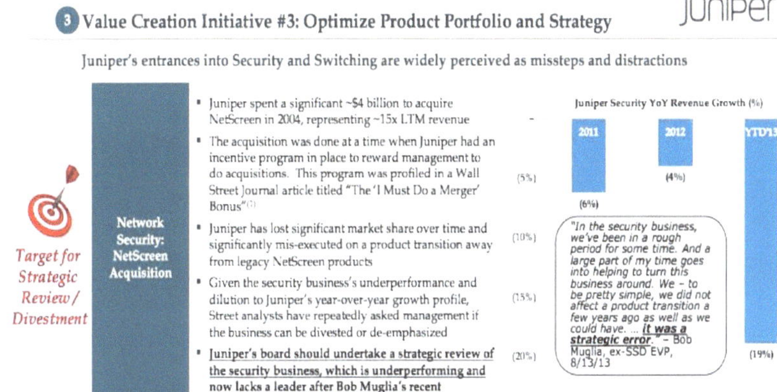

（华尔街著名对冲基金Elliott Management的调查报告）

对Juniper对NetScreen的收购基本上被公认为是一个失败收购。许多华尔街金融机构分析师在2013年就很尖锐提出了批评。

"On the product portfolio side, is there an argument that Juniper should be somewhat more focused?" – Credit Suisse, CS Tech Conference (12/4/13)

"Juniper's current product cycle ramp seems to be the result of efforts to out-innovate the competition beyond what the business organization structure could support. Juniper seems to have been committed to product launches while Cisco abandoned its strategy of innovation for a much more focused approach. Juniper's diversification in multiple new product segments could bring its relevance to its core customer base into question" – FBR (9/18/13)

"The Security business has been a very difficult one. ... Is that a core business for Juniper? Or could it be a candidate for divestiture at some point?" – Citigroup, Citi Global Technology Conference (9/4/13)

"We wonder if a new CEO would initiate a restructuring. Specifically, we believe that the company has too many products that continue to underperform, especially on the security side" – Stifel Nicolaus (8/20/13)

"Juniper has been donating market share in security for several years now implying a new strategic direction may be considered" – RBC (8/12/13)

"In security, Juniper has been trying to stabilize the business for some time. You have $2.8 billion in cash, which incidentally is the check that Cisco wrote this morning to acquire Sourcefire. So with that in mind, how do you accelerate change for the security division with the limited resources? And is the stability in the business worth all the investments that you're making or is it better to kind of reallocate those resources and refocus on wireless, core routers or PTX, which is your traditional areas of strength" – RBC, Q2'13 Earnings Call (7/23/13)

"Is it possible to separate [enterprise security] from the carrier security side and sort of run it for cash as opposed to for growth?" – Morgan Stanley, Q2'13 Earnings Call (7/23/13)

Elliott Management基金认为，Juniper必须迅速整改，改变产品线结构，聚焦。对NetScreen产品线和后来发展的SRX产品线，需要调整。

这份重量级的调查报告直接导致了后来Juniper的一些重大业务调整，NetScreen产品线之后被合并进入了交换机产品线，一些非重要的安全产品项目被暂停或者撤销。

在M&A方面，Juniper与经验老道的Cisco差距非常大。Cisco过去许多年的发展都是通过收购获得新的产品，然后利用其强大的销售渠道，占领市场。但缺乏经验的Juniper收购NeteScreen之后，试图迅速的把NetScreen的ScreenOS软件系统整合到Juniper的软件系统中JUNOS中去。这是一个重大的战略错误。Juniper的管理层在2000年初没有深刻的认识到网络安全是一个独立的行业。而网络安全本身是一个巨大的行业在10年之后的2010年得到了广泛的证明。例如，从NetScreen分离出来的PaloAlto Networks的市值现在已经超过了Juniper整个公司本身。

Conclusion & Next Steps　　JUNIPER

- **This three-pronged value plan outlines a "New Juniper" - with a streamlined cost structure, a capital return plan and a strategic review of the product portfolio - all of which we strongly believe will be readily embraced by our fellow shareholders:**
    1. Cost realignment: $200M operating expense reduction implemented over 2014
    2. Capital return: $3.5B share repurchase program over 2 years with a $2.5B ASR immediately and a $1.0B ASR in 2015 and an ongoing commitment to return 50% of free cash flow including a $0.125 quarterly dividend
    3. Product portfolio optimization: Conduct strategic review of security and switching businesses to simplify Juniper's product portfolio to focus on projects with the greatest risk-adjusted return on investment
- We recommend immediate implementation of these three recommended value creation initiatives with appropriate messaging and detail
- Proper messaging of these new highly value-accretive initiatives will convey to the market that this value creation plan is actually a transformation and that Juniper is on a new, sustainable path towards consistent value-maximization
- **We sincerely hope that we can work with management and the board in a friendly and collaborative manner to institute the necessary changes and put Juniper back on the path towards success**
- **We thank Juniper for consideration of these thoughts**

Juniper has an incredible opportunity to deliver long-overdue value to shareholders through the three-pronged plan, which we believe can lead to a stock price of $35-$40 per share

（Elliott Management基金对Juniper调查的总结）

Single JUNOS战略的困惑

Juniper公司有一个非常重要的，一直强调和坚持的战略：Single JUNOS。相比于Cisco有多个网络操作系统同时在市面上部署， Juniper只研发和维护一个网络管理操作系统JUNOS，从而使得其客户的TCO（Total Cost of Ownership）最小。Juniper的这个战略极大影响了Juniper对NetScreen公司，和其后来通过M&A收购的公司的产品和系统的集成节奏。后来的事实证明，Juniper的Single JUNOS公司战略没有在进入要求灵活多变，迅速发布的企业市场后及时调整，可能是导致NetScreen收购后集成的缓慢，滞后和整体被华尔街和网络界公认为是一个不成功的案例， 和Juniper过去10年来公司各方面被动的重要原因之一，例如，Juniper在收购NetScreen后，立刻停止了

NeteScreen的ScreenOS和已经就绪流片的ASIC的若干个研发计划，态度非常坚决的要迅速的把ScreenOS的安全功能移植到JUNOS上，简单的把安全当作是路由的一个附加服务。这一重大决策导致了Juniper/NetScreen错过了宝贵的4年时光（SRX 5800直到2008年9月，也就是收购之后的4年才推出）。4年的时光，使得NetScreen在企业市场，特别是企业网络安全方向的先机消失殆尽。这是一个非常值得反思的事情。直到十年之后的今天，Juniper才真正理解网络安全本身是一个行业，而且是一个巨大的行业。

Juniper坚持Single JUNOS的战略是有其历史根源的。Juniper公司创办于1996年。创办之初的目的就是要与Cisco开展竞争，并从运营商市场的边缘路由器（Edge Router）开始发力。Juniper为了在市场上很好的定位自己，以区别于Cisco，一个重要的战略就是极力提倡其基于FreeBSD的JUNOS系统软件。JUNOS改写了FreeBSD的网络协议栈部分，如TCP/IP stack和相关路由协议，以及用户界面，增加了不少硬件模块管理部分等，各个功能模块都是独立的Unix进程。可以说，与IOS相比，JUNOS是一个更加稳定可靠的网络OS，例如，一个模块的Bug不会影响其他模块的运行，系统比较稳定也比较容易调试。另外，JUNOS可以进行不停机的功能升级。从用户的角度来看，IOS和JUNOS的用户界面类似，都是使用所谓的CLI（Commend Line Interface）；在网络功能上，都支持标准的协议，MPLS，RIP，OSPF，BGP，VPN等等。在一个统一的JUNOS系统软件下，Juniper的所有的硬件系统上，特别是在起家的路由器产品M系列，T系列，都运行着一个有严格版本控制的JUNOS。在产品发布方面，因为绝大多数是运营商客户，采取了严格的定期的版本发布流程（每三个月一个发布）。

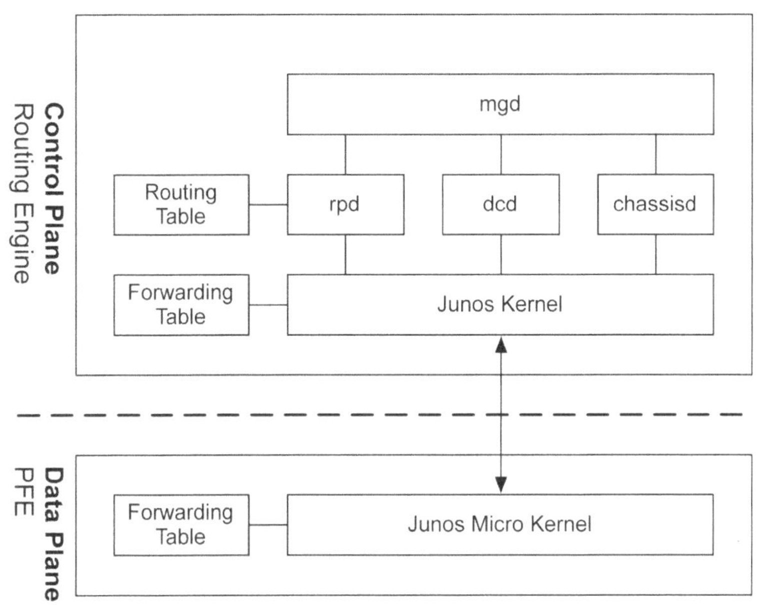

（Juniper的JUNOS体系结构）

如上图JUNOS逻辑体系结构可见，JUNOS分为两大部分，基于FreeBSD的RE(Routing Engine)部分，和报文转发的PFE(Packet Forward Engine)部分。狭义上的JUNOS是指RE部分。各个Juniper的路由器上的基于x86的管理平台上都运行着一个统一的JUNOS。各个系统平台的报文处理部分可以有略微不同的PFE部分。PFE通常是指硬件ASIC，或者说，线卡部分的控制软件。

Juniper的这种单一网络操作系统的策略在公司的早期发展过程中，获得了很大的成功，特别是对需要安全可靠，稳定的运营商客户群。用户可以购买各种系列的产品，但管理平台都是一个相同的JUNOS/RE。这种策略大大降低了用户网络的管理成本，逐步成为Juniper公司的一个亮点，成为公司的CEO层面，市场宣传层面的一个重要组成部分--Single JUNOS，降低客户的TCO。

Juniper的竞争对手Cisco方面，确实一直存在着多个操作系统的困惑。也曾经试图统一规整，但似乎都没有成功。Cisco最开始起家的操作系统叫做IOS，被广泛的安装在早期的交换机产品线上；在核心路由器CRS-1推出后，推出的操作系统是IOS XR(基于QNX的Neutrino微内核)。之后，Cisco推出重要的边缘路由器ASR 1000产品。其上面的操作系统是IOS XE(可以在Linux上模拟多个IOS进程)。在数据中心产品方面，Cisco的旗舰网络交换机Nexus交换机的操作系统是NX-OS(基于Monta Vista的Embedded Linux)。

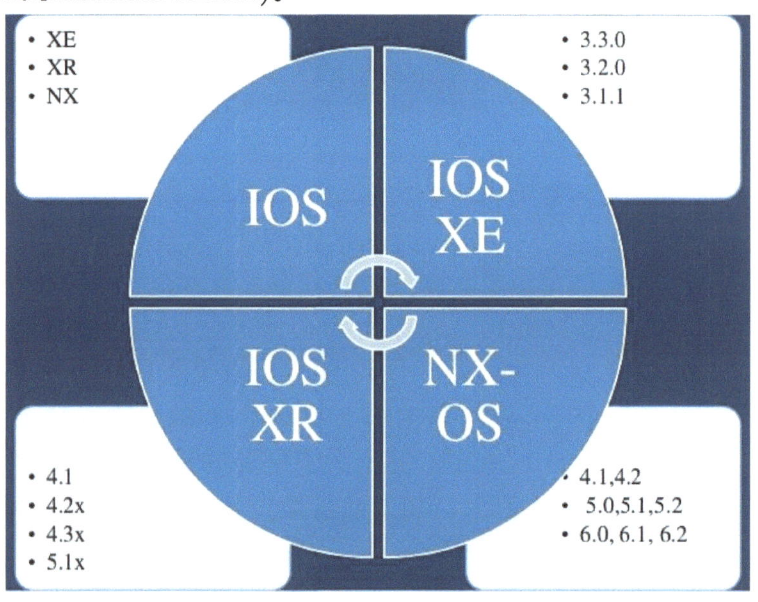

（思科的多OS战略）

Networking Software Systems

IOS

- Integrates technology, business services, and hardware support
- Reduces operational spending
- Optimizes return on investment
- Improves business productivity

IOS XE

- Supports next-generation platforms
- Runs as a single daemon within a modern Linux operating system
- Separates the data plane and control plane
- Improved services integration

IOS XR

- Focuses on the needs of service providers
- Designed for the dynamic network usage requirements of services
- Flexible programmability for dynamic reconfiguration

NX-OS

- Open, modular and programmable for an agile data center infrastructure
- Optimized for both physical and virtual data center deployments
- Highly reliable continuous system operation, optimizing uptime

（思科的多OS应用于不同的市场方向）

研发和维护多个操作系统的缺点增加用户的维护成本和学习时间，也就是通常所说的TCO。这是Juniper公司一直试图“攻击”Cisco的地方。

我们认为，在Juniper早期，公司的创立，发展期间，极力打Single JUNOS的牌是正确的选择。获得了在运营商市场激烈竞争环境中生存下来的空间和时间。但是从过去这些年的市场数据来看，我们也可以有趣的认识到思科公司的多个网络OS方案似乎并未使思科丢失市场份额。

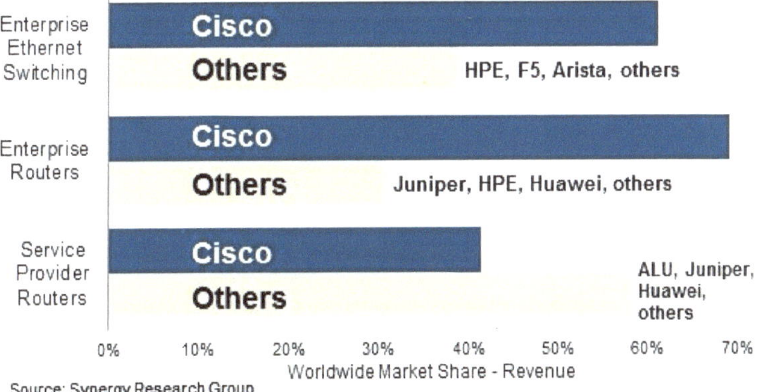

（2015年4季度交换机和路由器的市场份额分布图）

从2015年的交换机和路由器市场份额数据，我们可以看见，Cisco在企业交换机市场，企业路由器市场，运营商市场都还是占了绝对领导的地位。
理论上讲，对于一家网络设备厂商来说，研发和维护一个OS要好于多个OS。但是，为什么思科放弃了统一IOS，而是采用了多个操作系统的"Train"的方案，并从而在市场份额上持续保持领先呢？
我们认为在John Chambers领导下的思科赢在了对需要灵活多变的企业级产品市场的深刻理解上；赢在了对收购一个中小型网络公司之后，如何持续保持一个具备旺盛生命力的公司的创新能力，如何持续的占有市场份额上。占领市场份额的优先级大于内部整合的优先级。
Juniper收购NetScreen的最重要的战略目标是进入企业级产品市场，通过网络安全，切入企业产品线，然后带动企业交换机的交叉销售，从而为Juniper公司带来新的营业额增长点。但是，因为Juniper的管理层不敢轻易放弃Signle JUNOS的市场战略，导致了采取僵化的方案：放弃了迅速利用NetScreen灵活多变的ScreenOS研发和发布方案，转为花费4年的移植ScreenOS的安全功能（FLOW）到JUNOS上，导致了市场上，丧失了在企业网络安全市场上的先发优势；在研发上，直到2008年才推出SRX产品线。
如果历史能够重演，正确的做法应该是：收购NetScreen后，迅速利用Juniper的渠道，NetScreen现有的渠道，大力进入企业网络产品市场，迅速形成交叉销售。同时，立刻更新当时NetScreen的主力产品NS5000系统，ISG2000系统（含IDP）。逐步扩大和稳定住NetScreen在中高端网络安全产品市场的领导地位。如果Juniper当年这样去理解企业网，安全产品，这个世界上的网络安全产业可能就会被重写。
反观思科对收购公司的战略，业界普遍认为非常成功。其一贯战略是迅速的利用强大的销售渠道，持续的产生销售，持续扩大市场份额。然后在集团整体的布局下，采纳了多个火车Train的研发和市场战略，不同的业务方向，采纳不同的操作系统。从过去的发展来看，多个Train的研发方向，例如，传统企业交换机的IOS，高端路由器的IOS XR；边缘路由器的IOS XE；数据中心交换机的NOX-OS并没有成为思科的负担。思科如何处理M&A的策略深深值得Juniper和未来的高科技公司领导人深思。

安全是一个独立的信息行业

2004年，当Juniper并购NetScreen的时候，由于Juniper是一个传统的网络公司，更具体一点，是一个为运营商提供MPLS路由交换的公司，对Ethernet，对企业网，对网络安全缺乏深刻的认识。Juniper的高层误判Security是Network的一种附加值(Value Added)服务，而非安全本身是一个独立的行业。这也是Juniper在收购NetScreen之后迅速停止了NetScreen的一些重大产品和芯片研发，而把重点放在了把NetScreen产品中的安全功能剥离出来，并整合到Juniper的路由产品上的原因。

事实证明，从2004年以来的发展到2016年的今天，安全产业的发展不仅仅是一个信息产业的一个细分行业，而是一个独立和巨大的行业。CyberSecurity已经成为世界上各个大国的国家战略；国家之间博弈的重要组成部分。

2004年以来，安全工业界的演变日新月异，从传统的FW和IDS盒子，演变到下一代NGFW，APT。从传统基于规则的软硬件防火墙，到基于机器学习的威胁感知，应用业务可视化；从传统的企业边界安全，到移动安全，IoT设备安全，演变到Endpoint安全，云安全；从传统的日志SIEM系统到基于数据分析的日志加报文的统一分析引擎；从传统的报文过滤安全，到完整的智能数据安全方案。一个巨大的，独立于传统网络行业的数据安全行业已经形成，而且成为现代数字社会的重要基础组成部分。例如，以CheckPoint, PaloAlto Networks为代表的NGFW公司，截至2016年12月31日，CheckPoint市值是147亿美金；PaloAlto市值是114亿美金。而Juniper才是107亿美金。从日志SIEM市场演变过来的大数据分析安全公司Splunk也是69亿美金。随着移动互联网，大数据，人工智能，IoT行业的发展，安全已经成为一个越来越重要的基础设施，成为任何一个新兴行业要能够落地的重要前提条件。例如，如果安全问题解决不好，移动金融业，无人驾驶汽车，智能家庭，大规模公有云，都无从谈起。

安全行业一个令工业界，华尔街高度重视的特征是：一直在不断的迅速的变化着。新问题层出不穷。每隔2，3年，安全行业就都会有一些重大的整合，重大的新问题，新机遇。特别是与其他新兴行业的结合。这一点非常有别于传统的网络交换和路由行业。

从市场调查公司MarketsandMarkets的数据显示，整体安全市场的大小在2021年会高达2千零20亿（202 Billion)美金。CAGR为10.6%。其中应用安全将会是未来最大的爆发和机会成长点。“Application security to grow at the highest CAGR from 2016 to 2021 Cyber security solutions are used to secure the network infrastructure and the devices connected through it...... Application security is expected to witness the highest CAGR in the global cyber security market during the period 2016–2021.”。而以此同时，从Grand View Research在2016年的一份研究报告中，我们发现，在路由器和交换机市场，到2022年，市场调查数据显示，市场大小为420亿美金。

安全不是网络的一个附加服务是一个非常重要的认识；安全本身是一个不断变化的，日新月异的行业。如果网络交换有一天会成为commodity产品，例如，随着SDN的软件定义网络的冲击，安全产业不会沦落。安全的问题只会随着人类数字文明的进步，变得更复杂，也更重要。

第七章 烟云演变

NetScreen被收购10年后，当年的创办人，管理团队，研发和市场人员逐渐离开了Juniper，创办了自己的基金，创业公司或者融入了硅谷的其他高科技公司。在硅谷，在美国网络安全界，NetScreen的同事们互相提携，互相帮助，逐渐发展成为一个“NetScreen圈子”，影响着世界范围的网络安全产业的发展。
下面是与NetScreen圈子紧密相关的一些企业或机构的考察。

北极光创投

由NetScreen创办人邓锋与柯严共同创办于2004年末，是一个致力于科技，医疗，能源等方面的，一个聚焦中国产业环境的风险投资公司。

邓锋和柯严分别于2004年下半年低调离开Juniper，并开始在投资领域发展。北极光创投创办以来，投资了许多著名的公司，例如，展讯，汉庭，美团，中科创达等。

“北极光创投是一家以“扶持世界级的中国企业家，培育世界级的中国企业”为宗旨的风险投资机构。创立于2005年的北极光的创投，伴随着高速发展的中国经济快速成长。目前，旗下管理资产总额近500亿人民币。北极光创投的投资机构来自美国、欧洲和亚洲的一流大学捐赠基金、主权基金、家族基金、慈善基金以及国内最优秀的政府背景的母基金等。北极光先后在高科技，新媒体，通讯（TMT），清洁技术，消费及健康医疗等领域投资逾百家公司。”

飞塔网络（NASDAQ：FTNT）

由NetScreen创办人谢青创办于2000年［注：谢青1999年10月离开NetScreen］，是一个与NetScreen提供类似网络安全产品的公司，但更聚焦在AV，IPS，Firewall集成在一起的UTM系统。其主打产品是基于ASIC／FPGA的高端系统。Fortinet于2009年在NASDAQ上市，目前市值为50多亿美金。

艾诺威科技［NASDAQ：HIVE］

由NetScreen早期员工，网络部门负责人Changming Liu创办于2006年。是一家提供智能无线产品和解决方案的高科技公司。"Aerohive developed a controller-less wireless LAN architecture called Cooperative Control, which provides all the performance, availability, management, mobility, and security needed in a large campus deployment, and, with the elimination of controllers in the architecture, is appropriate even in small branch office and warehouse deployments. This controller-less architecture also enables secure, scalable, high-performance, and mission-critical wireless networking in a manageable and cost-effective way to industries such as education, healthcare, state and local government, manufacturing, distribution, and retail."

Aerohive是由北极光创投投资和长期支持下创办，成长，并在2014年3月成功在NYSE上市。目前市值为2.93亿美金。

AeroHive目前的CEO是NetScreen期间管理团队里的市场副总裁David Flynn。

PaloAlto Networks Inc[NASDAQ: PANW]

the network security company

2005年，由NetScreen收购的公司OneSecure的创办人，后出任NetScreen CTO的Nir Zuk主要创办，其他还有若干个联合创办人。其中之一为Yuming Mao，NetScreen的早期员工，ATG组的负责人。PaloAlto Networks主要是研发下一代防火墙(NGFW)的高科技公司。2012年7月，PaloAlto Networks成功在美国NASDAQ上市。目前市值140亿美金。**令人感慨的事情是，PaloAlto Networks是从Juniper的NetScreen产品线分离出来，若干年后成功上市，现在的市值已经超过了Juniper。**PaloAlto Networks目前的研发总裁Wilson Xu也是NetScreen的早期员工。另外一个很有趣的现象是，PaloAlto Networks公司是前NetScreen／Juniper网络与安全产品线员工最多的一家公司。

山石网科

由NetScreen研发部门骨干，早期员工，平台部门负责人Jacson Tong，ASIC部门负责人 Dongping Luo，VPN部门负责人Tim Liu，SME部门负责人Ning Mo，Flow组骨干Zhong Wang等创

办。主要是研发和提供硬件高性能防火墙。 Hillstone创办以来一直得到北极光创投的资金支持。目前市场方向主要是聚焦中国市场，在北京，苏州和硅谷都有研发中心。

杰华科技

SIGMA Silicon Valley Test Experts

由NetScreen研发部门骨干，早期员工，QA部门负责人Ting Tan等人创办。成立于 2005 年 4 月，中国区三个研发中心分布于成都、北京、杭州，同时投资建立了 16 个专业实验室。杰华科技为客户提供“向全球市场交付高品质的外包服务和专业解决方案”，向客户提供高性价比的高端测试服务、人员外包、测试脚本开发、测试产品与工具的开发和销售、测试咨询服务，以及面向高校和企业人员的测试培训与认证服务。

vArmour Networks Inc

vARMOUR

由NetScreen研发部门骨干，早期员工，ScreenOS部门负责人Roger Lian，VPN部门负责人Michael Shieh联合创办。主要是研发和提供云安全的虚拟防火墙系统。目前总共已经得到许多重量级VC的投资。发展迅猛，公司估值已经多达4亿美金。vArmour公司许多骨干员工也都是NetScreen／Juniper网络与安全产品线的员工。

Niara Inc

Niara是一个基于大数据分析的网络安全公司，聚焦于APT检测和相关报警和策略控制。创办于2013年10月，创办人是前NetScreen收购的SSL／VPN公司负责人之一，后来成为Juniper网络安全产品线研发副总裁的SRIRAM RAMACHANDRAN。Niara目前获得了NEA和Venrock等硅谷著名大公司的投资。

CloudPassage

NetScreen的前CEO，Robert Thomas，出任NetScreen 1999-2004年的CEO，期间带领公司上市。在Juniper收购NetScreen之后，迅速的离开Juniper，加入了InfoBlox (NYSE: BLOX)，并成功的带领InfoBlox发展壮大，并在NYSE上市。目前市值为8.9亿美金。Robert Thomas在InfoBlox工作十年。2015年1月离开加入CloudPassage出任CEO。

Arista Networks

NetScreen的前销售副总裁，Mark Smith，一直负责NetScreen 1999年7月到2004年4月的销售。之后跟随前CEO加盟InfoBlox出任销售的EVP。目前是Artista Networks的SVP，负责Arista Networks的全球销售业务。

Illumio

Illumio是一个为企业，私有云或者公有云提供安全可视化，特别是微隔离的安全可视化，安全策略管理和控制的初创公司。创办人PJ Kirner是前NetScreen/Juniper安全产品线的高级架构师。另外，Illumio的CFO是NetScreen上市时的CFO REMO CANESSA。Illumio创办以来获得了许多著名VC的投资，融资额已经达到1.42亿美金。其中包括Andreessen Horowitz, Accel Partners。另外也有一些著名的个人投资者投资了Illumio，其中包括微软的董事会主席John W. Thompson, Salesforce的CEO Marc Benioff和Yahoo的创办人之一杨致远。

参考文献

NetScreen Technologies
https://en.wikipedia.org/wiki/NetScreen_Technologies
NetScreen Technologies @ Crunchbase
https://www.crunchbase.com/organization/netscreen-technologies
NetScreenn IPO S-1 Form
http://www.nasdaq.com/markets/ipos/filing.ashx?filingid=1560878
ScreenOS Wiki https://en.wikipedia.org/wiki/ScreenOS
ScreenOS Concepts & Examples ScreenOS Reference Guide
http://www.juniper.net/techpubs/software/screenos/screenos6.3.0/630_ce_all.pdf
Efficient Networks & NetScreen Tech Acquisition
http://www.wsj.com/articles/SB95425657366629179
NetScreen & OneSecure Acquisition Press Release
http://www.sec.gov/Archives/edgar/data/1088454/000101287002003981/dex9901.txt
NetScreen & Neoteris Acquisition Press Release
http://www.sec.gov/Archives/edgar/data/1088454/000119312503058242/dex991.htm
Juniper Networks Wiki
https://en.wikipedia.org/wiki/Juniper_Networks
Juniper & NetScreen Acquisition Press Release
Juniper & NetScreen Acquisition SEC Filing
http://www.sec.gov/Archives/edgar/data/1088454/000119312504063819/d425.htm
Juniper Networks--Elliott Management's Perspectives
http://www.valuewalk.com/wp-content/uploads/2014/01/JuniperJanuary.pdf

Juniper Networks SEC Filings
http://investor.juniper.net/investor-relations/sec-filings/default.aspx
Northern Light Venture Capital http://www.nlvc.com
Fortinet Networks http://www.fortinet.com
AeroHive Networks http://www.aerohive.com
Hillstone Networks http://www.hillstonenet.com
PaloAlto Networks https://www.paloaltonetworks.com
http://www.grandviewresearch.com/industry-analysis/global-router-and-switch-market
http://www.marketsandmarkets.com/Market-Reports/cyber-security-market-505.html

附录一，NetScreen公司大事编年考

1997年10月30日 NetScreen 公司成立，创办人为邓锋（Deng Feng），柯严（Ke Yan）和谢青（Xie Qing）

1998年1月2日 Internet Domain "netscreen.com" 注册.

1998年6月，NetScreen推出其NetScreen-100和NetScreen-10网络安全产品。

1998年8月，NetScreen推出其NetScreen-Remote VPN Client网络系统软件。

1998年10月，Robert Thomas加入NetScreen Tech Inc.并出任CEO & President。其时NetScreen Inc.员工为38人。32人为来自中国的工程师。

1999年9月，谢青，NetScreen三共同创始人之一，离开NetScreen。

1999年9月，NetScreen推出其NetScreen-Global Manager 网络管理系统软件。

1999年9月，NetScreen推出其NetScreen-5网络安全产品。

1999年11月，NetScreen完成并推出其第一代GigaScreen ASIC。

1999年9月，NetScreen推出其NetScreen-Global Manager 网络管理系统软件。

1999年，NetScreen员工人数达 45人。

2000年3月28日，Efficient Networks Inc.(NASDAQ：EFNT)宣布以9亿5百9十万美金的股票交换收购NetScreen。

2000年5月4日，NetScreen发布ScreenOS操作系统2.0。

2000年5月，NetScreen推出其GigaScreen ASIC Based NetScreen-1000网络安全产品。

2000年6月5日，Efficient Networks(Nasdaq: EFNT) and NetScreen联合宣布取消之前的购买合并计划。

2000年9月18日，，NetScreen发布ScreenOS操作系统2.1。

2000年12月18日， NetScreen发布ScreenOS操作系统2.5。
2000, NetScreen员工人数达180人。总卖出设备量为15140台。
2001年2月22日， 西门子(Siemens)出价15亿美金收购Efficient Networks公司。Efficient曾于2000年试图以9.1亿美金的价格收购NetScreen。
2001年3月，NetScreen推出其NetScreen-Global Pro Manager 网络管理系统软件。
2001年4月30日， NetScreen发布ScreenOS操作系统2.6。
2001年5月，NetScreen推出其NetScreen-500网络安全产品。
2001年6月，NetScreen推出其NetScreen-5XP网络安全产品。
2001年6月，NetScreen完成并推出其第二代GigaScreen ASIC。
2001年9月10日， NetScreen发布ScreenOS操作系统2.7。
2001年9月30日，NetScreen员工为332名。其中96研发(R&D)人员；149名销售和市场人员。30名客户支持，和57名管理和运营人员。
2001年10月1日， NetScreen发布ScreenOS操作系统3.0。
2001年10月5日，正式提交SEC S-1文件。
2001年11月，NetScreen推出其NetScreen-25/50网络安全产品。
2001年12月12日, NASDAQ IPO. 股票代号为NSCN。以每股16美金的价格在NASDAQ股票市场公开发售1千万(10 Million)股票。开盘价23.76美金; 收盘价23.72美金. 公司市值为15亿9千4百万美金. 公司员工330人。
2001年12月28日， NetScreen发布ScreenOS操作系统2.8。
2001, NetScreen员工人数达329人。总卖出设备量为43915台。
2002年1月2日， NetScreen发布ScreenOS操作系统3.1。
2002年1月，NetScreen推出NetScreen-204/208网络安全产品。
2002年4月15日，NetScreen推出其GigaScreen ASIC II Based NetScreen-5200网络安全产品。

2002年6月20日，邓锋与柯严同时获得著名的Ernst & Young北加州地区2002年度企业家荣誉。
2002年6月25日，NetScreen的NetScreen-1000产品获得Frost & Sullivan评选的2002年度产品发明工程奖。NetScreen-1000是工业界第一个达到千兆位(Gigabit)数据处理速度的防火墙产品。
2002年8月1日，NetScreen发布ScreenOS操作系统4.0。
2002年8月22日，NetScreen Inc. 以$40.3 million收购OneSecure Inc. OneSecure创办人Nir Zuk出任NetScreen CTO。
2002年9月18日，NetScreen Inc. 完成对OneSecure Inc.收购。
2002年9月30日，NetScreen员工为493名。其中149研发(R&D)人员；225名销售和市场人员。35名客户支持，和84名管理和运营人员。
2002年9月，NetScreen推出NetScreen Remote网络安全产品。
2002年9月，NetScreen推出NetScreen-IDP 100网络安全产品。
2002年10月，NetScreen推出GigaScreen ASIC II Based NetScreen 5400网络安全产品。
2002年11月，NetScreen推出NetScreen-IDP 500网络安全产品。
2003年2月10日，NetScreen总部从位从350 Oakmead Parkway Sunnyvale, California迁址于805 11th Ave., Sunnyvale, California, USA。占地约156,000平方英尺。
2003年3月12日，NetScreen宣布，根据著名的Infonetics Research机构对2002年第4季度全球防火墙和VPN市场分额调查报告，NetScreen高端网络安全产品(售价超过3万美金的系统)占据第一，拥有33%的市场分额。在2002年第3季度，NetScreen高端产品的分额为28%。
2003年7月1日，NetScreen宣布，根据著名的Infonetics Research机构对2003年第1季度全球防火墙和VPN市场分额调查报告，NetScreen高端网络安全产品(售价超过3万美金的系统)继续占据第一，拥有32+%的市场分额。 在中端产品(售价位1万到3万美金之间)上，NetScreen占据17%的分额为全球第二。在全球总体网络安全产品销售分额上，排名第三。

2003年7月7日，NetScreen向业界展示其安全产品对IPV6的支持和承诺。

2003年8月18日，NetScreen宣布中国联通(China Unicom)选择购买其安全产品。

2003年9月12日，邓锋被著名的CRN杂志评选为2003年25位发明创造者(Innovator)荣誉获得者之一。同时入选的还有Google Inc.的创办人Sergey Brin和Larry Page。

2003年9月17日，NetScreen宣布，根据著名的Infonetics Research机构对2003年第2季度全球防火墙和VPN的市场分额调查研究报告，NetScreen在全球总体网络安全产品(Firewall/VPN)销售量(Unit)分额上，排名第二。

2003年9月30日，NetScreen员工为646名。其中181研发(R&D)人员；277名销售和市场人员。75名客户支持，和113名管理和运营人员。

2003年10月6日，NetScreen宣布以10.9million股票和20million现金的方式收购Neoteris Inc.。

2003年10月，NetScreen完成并推出其第三代GigaScreen ASIC.

2003年11月17日，NetScreen宣布完成对Neoteris公司的收购。

2003年12月9日，Anson Chen, 原Cisco Intelligent Network Services Management Business Unit Vice President & General Manager, 加入NetScreen Inc.出任VP of Engineering。邓锋转任Chief Strategy Officer(CSO)。

2003年12月18日，NetScreen发布ScreenOS操作系统5.0。

2003年12月31日，NetScreen员工为859人。

2004年2月9日，Juniper(JNPR)以NSCN股票2月6日市值26.40美金为基点，出价约40亿美金并购NetScreen。

2004年3月17日，NetScreen宣布其赢得VARBusiness杂志对北美信息技术设备公司在销售渠道合作方面等的5星级的评估。

2004年4月6日，NetScreen宣布SWIFT在3300台NetScreen-5XT设备的基础上，将计划在2004年底铺设多于10,000台。NetScreen 5XT设备来保护分布于200个国家的7500家金融机构。
2004年4月16日，NetScreen宣布推出GigaScreen-III ASIC based ISG2000产品。
2004年4月16日，JNPR和NSCN的股票拥有者各自批准了Juniper对NetScreen的并购。NSCN在NASDAQ正式消失。NetScreen股票持有人共占Juniper股票的24.5%。
2004年4月19日 Post-NetScreen Era。

后NetScreen时代

2004年4月19日，NetScreen的中国工程师进入Post-NetScreen时代（后Netscreen时代）。2004-2006年，经历了大批高层和骨干员工离开。之后，留下来的研发在各种压力下在2008年完成了高端系统SRX5000产品线的研发。并迅速延伸至中低端产品线。2010，2012年迎来了第2次的骨干团队的出走，Kernel Group和Flow Group骨干大面积离开。2013-2014年NetScreen留下最后的一些骨干遭到裁员。
2004年6月28日，原NetScreen CEO Robert Thomas离开Juniper。
2004年6月29日，原NetScreen CFO Remo Canessa离开Juniper。
2004年9月17日，原NetScreen VP of Engineering, Anson Chen, 离开Juniper。
2004年10月22日， Juniper SPG 发布ScreenOS操作系统5.1。
2004年11月15日，原NetScreen VP of Sales Mark Smith离开Juniper。
2005年2月1日，邓锋，原NetScreen Inc. Co-Founder, VP of Security Products strategy, Juniper, 正式转为Part-Time，结束其Juniper的全职工作。后低调全身退出Juniper。
2005年3月, NetScreen CTO, Nir Zuk离开Juniper。
2005年4月1日，原NetScreen QA Department Director Ting Tan离开Juniper。

2005年5月9日，Juniper SPG宣布推出GigaScreen III ASIC based ISG2000+IDP和ISG1000产品。

2005年5月11日， Juniper SPG 发布ScreenOS操作系统5.2。

2005年6月， 原Netscreen VP of Marketing, David Flynn, Left Absense。后悄然离开Juniper。

2005年6月14日，NetScreen ASIC R&D负责人， SPG Advanced Technology Center Director Wen Wei离开Juniper。

2005年8月22日，Dongping Luo宣布NetScreen GigScreen ASIC Jupiter-3X流片。

2005年10月1日， 柯严， Co-Founder of NetScreen Inc., VP of SME Product Line, Chief Architect, SPG, Juniper, 离开Juniper。

2005年10月24日，Juniper SPG发布ScreenOS操作系统5.3。

2006年2月17日， 原NetScreen Founding Engineer, Juniper DE, Chief Architect of SPG SME Engineering, Yuming Mao离开Juniper加入和参与创办PaloAlto Networks。

2006年2月28日，原NetScreen网络部门负责人Changmin Liu, Juniper DE离开Juniper。

2006年4 18日， 原NetScreen ScreenOS Department Director Roger Lian离开Juniper。

2006年5月19日，SPG ScreenOS Department Infrastructure Group Manager, Jiawei Jang, 离开Juniper。

2006年7月24日， Juniper SPG发布ScreenOS操作系统5.4。

2006年9月11日， 根据Infonetics的研究报告，Juniper宣布其网络安全产品营业额在2006年第2季度排名第2。这是NetScreen安全产品历史上第一次从营业额的指标评比中占据全球第2的地位。另外，其高端防火墙产品系列在营业额和卖出数量方面皆超过Cisco. 在SSL/VPN方面，依旧保持第1的位置。在安全路由(Secure Routing)方面， 占据第3，其ScreenOS为操作系统的SSG产品系列获得了成功。在IDP方面位居第4。

2006 年9月14日，原NetScreen Board/System部门负责人，SME产品线负责人，中国研发中心总负责人， Jian Tong， 离开Juniper。
2006年9月22日，原NetScreen GigaScreen ASIC的主要贡献者之一， Juniper SPG Advanced Technology Center Senior Manager, Dongping Luo, 离开Juniper。
2006年10月6日，原NetScreen SME产品线 Senior Manager, Ning Mo, 离开Juniper。
2006年10月13日， SPG VPN Group Senior Manager, Tim Liu, 离开Juniper。
2007年4月19日, Juniper发布ScreenOS 6.0。
2008年1月28日, Juniper发布ScreenOS 6.1。
2008年11月7日, Juniper发布ScreenOS 6.2。
2008年6月30日, NetScreen NS25/50, NS500 End of Life.不再对外提供发货。
2008年9月15日, Juniper发布世界上最高端的防火墙系统SRX5800系列。
2008年9月30日, NetScreen NS5XT, NS204/208 End of Life. 不再对外发货。
2008年12月31日, NetScreen NS5G End of Life. 不再对外发货。
2009年3月9日, Juniper发布SRX 3000系列。
2009年9月1日, Juniper发布ScreenOS 6.3 //最后一个发布
2010年4月1日, Juniper网络安全产品线Kernel Group负责人Huailin Chen离开Juniper。
2012年9月3日, Juniper网络安全产品线SRX系统和Flow Group重要负责人Dongyi Jiang, Jin Shang离开Juniper。
2013年2月, Juniper北京研发中心负责人Frank Zou因为Juniper机构调整离开Juniper。
2013年2月, Juniper网络安全产品平台部研发总监Shuhua Ge因为Juniper机构调整离开Juniper。

2013年2月, Juniper北京研发中心平台部负责责人Qiuyuan Liu因为Juniper机构调整离开Juniper。
2014年1月13日, Hedge Fund Ellio发布关于Juniper的分析报告,其中关于NetScreen的收购被定义为失败和可惜了这个产品线。
2014年4月, Juniper网络安全产品平台部, DE Edward Ping因为Juniper机构调整离开Juniper。
2014年4月, Juniper网络安全产品平台部研发总监Jiaxiang Su因为Juniper机构调整离开Juniper。
2014年1月13日, 华尔街著名对冲基金Ellio发布关于Juniper的分析和整改报告,其中关于NetScreen的收购被定义为失败和并为之可惜. 其原文为："Pure-play security vendors today have a combined market cap of ~$30B. NetScreen was a leader and would have been more valuable and successful had it not lost share under Juniper's ownership"
2014年8月, Juniper网络安全产品线正式并入交换机产品和解决方案产品线。简称S3 BU。这个调整正式宣告NetScreen产品线的正式结束。

附录二， NetScreen投资机构（人）完整列表

GE Capital Equity Investments, Inc.
120 Long Ridge Road
Stamford, CT 06977
Scudder Technology Innovation Fund
c/o Zurich Scudder Investments, Inc.
345 Park Avenue
New York, NY 10154
Scudder Technology Fund
c/o Zurich Scudder Investments, Inc.
345 Park Avenue
New York, NY 10154
Capital Guardian US Small Capitalization Fund (Private Placement Eligible) for Tax Exempt Trusts c/o Capital Guardian Trust Company
630 Fifth Avenue, 36th Floor
New York, NY 10111-0121
With a copy to:
c/o Capital Guardian Trust Company
11100 Santa Monica Blvd., 15th Floor
Los Angeles, CA 90025-3384
Capital Guardian US Small Capitalization Master Fund (Private Placement Eligible)
c/o Capital Guardian Trust Company
630 Fifth Avenue, 36th Floor
New York, NY 10111-0121
With a copy to:
c/o Capital Guardian Trust Company
11100 Santa Monica Blvd., 15th Floor

Los Angeles, CA 90025-3384
Pennsylvania Public School Employees'
Retirement System
c/o Capital Guardian Trust Company
630 Fifth Avenue, 36th Floor
New York, NY 10111-0121
c/o Capital Guardian Trust Company
11100 Santa Monica Blvd., 15th Floor
Los Angeles, CA 90025-3384
SMALLCAP World Fund, Inc.
Los Angeles, CA 90071-1447
Spectrum Equity Investors IV, L.P.
Spectrum IV Investment Managers' Fund, L.P.
Menlo Park, CA 94025
Sequoia Capital VII
Sequoia Capital Franchise Fund
Sequoia Capital Franchise Partners
Sequoia Technology Partners VII
Sequoia International Partners
Sequoia 1997 LLC
SQP 1997
3000 Sand Hill Road
Bldg. 4, Suite 280
Menlo Park, CA 94025
Techgains Corporation
Techgains Pan Pacific Corporation
Techgains International Corporation
1111 Jupiter Rd. Suite 100B
Plano, TX 75074
Silicon Valley Equity Fund, L.P.

Silicon Valley Equity Fund II, L.P.
2041 Mission College Boulevard
Suite 100
Santa Clara, CA 95054
Technology Partners Venture Capital Corp. 2F-2, 130,
Szu-Wei Road
Hsinchu, Taiwan
Global Alliance Inc.
4-5, Tsukiji 1-Chome
Chuo-ku
Tokyo, 104-0045 Japan
KJL Investment
Chiu Family Living Trust
Chiu Family Children's Trust
Chiu Family Charitable Remainder Unitrust 19163 Via
Tesoro Court
Saratoga, CA 95070
E92 Plus Group, PLC
St. James House
St James Road
Surbiton Surrey KTG 4QH
United Kingdom
Hitachi Seibu Software, Ltd.
Hitachi Systems & Services, Ltd.
4-16, Uchihonmachi 2-chome, Chuo-ku
Osaka, 540-0026, Japan
EICO, Inc.
1054 Yosemite Drive
Milpitas, CA 95035
PJ&K Investments Corporation

2F-2, No. 130, Szu-Wei Road
Hsinchu, Taiwan
Nahil Sifri
2250, Place Transcanadienne
Dorval, (Quebec) H9P 2X5
Congress Communications, PLC
Wilshire House 19/21 Woolmead
Farnham Surrey GU9 OSJ
United Kingdom
Netsoft Associates
2727 Walsh Ave. Suite 101
Santa Clara, CA 95051
F & W Investments LLC
Two Palo Alto Square
Palo Alto, CA 94306
SecureSoft, Inc.
9th Floor, Doosan B/D,
105-7 Nonhyun-Dong,
Kangnam-Ku, Seoul, Korea
Case Technology, S.A.
Isla Del Hierro No.5,
28700 S.S. de Los Reyes, Madrid
Spain
Paul Gupta
15000 Blue Gum Court
Saratoga, CA 95070
Big Basin Partners, L.P.
14585 Big Basin Way
Saratoga, CA 95070
David C. Weng Living Trust

1101 Di Napoli Drive
San Jose, CA 95129
Sumitomo Corporation Tokyo
2-2, Hitotsubashi 1Chome
Chiyoda-ku, Tokyo
100-8601, Japan
TEKKANG Management Consulting Inc.
1111 S. Sherman Street #101
Richardson, TX 75081
Thomas F. and Kathy S. Mendoza
c/o Network Appliance, Inc.
495 East Java Drive
Sunnyvale, CA 94089
Hsun Kwei Chou and Aiko Chou Trust
13211 West Sunset Drive
Los Altos Hills, CA 94022
MCI WorldCom Venture Fund, Inc.
1801 Pennsylvania Ave, NW
Washington DC 20006
Ericsson Holding International B.V.
77 South Bedford St.
Burlington, Massachusetts 01803
Snaiso
141 Avenue de Veroun
92130 Issy-Les-Moolineaux
France
Daniel Gutenberg
Gutenberg Communications Systems AG
Hardturmstr. 101, CH-8005 Zurich
Equinox Solutions Through Partnership Ltd. Equinox House

25 Invincible Rd
Farnborough, Hampshire GU14 7QU
Presidio Venture Partners
2900 Patrick Henry Drive
Santa Clara CA 95054
Juniper Networks, Inc.
1194 North Mathilda Avenue
Sunnyvale, CA 94089
Datalink Business Solutions Ltd.
C1, 1F Phase 1,
Kaiser Estate
41 Man Yue St.
Hunghom Kowloon
Hong Kong
Cheng-FengChen
7th Floor, Room 3
#21, Sec. 2 Chung King So. Rd.
Taipei, Taiwan, ROC
Deacon Family Trust
884 Santa Rita Ave.
Los Altos, CA 94022
Hongping Zhang
3615 Rue Mirassou
San Jose, CA 95148
Michael M.C. Chiu
19163 Via Tesoro Ct.
Saratoga, CA 95070
CLAS Investment
4138 Remillard Court
Pleasanton, CA 94566

Yi-Chih Hans Tai
No. 4-1 Kou-Hwa Street
Hsinchu, Taiwan
Inkeun Lee
4701 NE Shore Place
Lake Forest Park, WA 98155
M. Liu Trust
1255 Post Street, Suite 840
San Francisco, CA 94109
Hien Ngoc Truong
1281 Arizona Ave.
Milpitas, CA 95035
Alex Chang
6048 Crossview Circle
San Jose, CA 95120
Godfrey Fong
12291 Barley Hill Road
Los Altos Hill, CA 94022
Comdisco, Inc.
6111 North River Road
Rosemount, Illinois 60018
GATX Ventures, Inc.

附录三，NetScreen月刊和相关图片资料

NetScreen从2000年11月，公司三周年的时候，开始发行内部的月刊，主要是每个月公司发生的一些大事，重要讲话，员工活动。2004年4月是最后一期。

非常有意思的是，NetScreen在2004年4月最后一期月刊上，采用的是第一期时CEO Robert Thomas在创刊时的照片--依在公司门前一棵大树前的眺望。

2000年12月创刊号的封面文章的题目是“Three Years Old--Where we be at Five？”。

2004年4月的最后一期的封面文章的题目是“The Last Chapter--or is it？”

这两篇类似社论文章的作者都是当时的CEO Robert Thomas。在2004年的告别文章里的最后一段话说道：

“We will find a good home at Juniper for our passion and our belief that we can do anything. We will go on to even bigger successes as a combined company. This is definitely not the last chapter--we haven’t even begun yet”

附录收集了NetScreen月刊里的一些具备纪念意义的照片和新闻事件，同时也收集了一些NetScreen员工当年的历史照片。

ScreenStories

NetScreen

November 2000, Volume 1

Three Years Old – Where Will We Be at Five?

It's been a pretty wild ride over the last three years and it's not over yet!

NetScreen's third birthday coincides almost exactly with my second anniversary in the company and I've seen enormous changes. I remember worrying about our first million dollar quarter and how difficult it seemed. I remember counting the pennies as we headed towards an empty bank account during our Series D funding round.

I also remember one of the tier one VCs (who, by the way, tried to screw us on price during that financing) telling me that channel development and loyalty would be a major problem for us and that the NetScreen-1000 would not be a significant part of our product line. He had just been through a funding round with RAMP Networks and he was very bullish about their future because they had solved that channel problem.

Well, today RAMP has a market capitalization of about $40 million and in their last published quarter (June 30) recorded revenues of just $5.8 million compared with NetScreen's $8.8 million. The September quarter will see an even bigger difference between the two companies and NetScreen's "market capitalization" is many times that of RAMP. How the world changes!

And, channel loyalty is definitely not an issue for us. We held an event in Monterey last week for our top 25 partners and the amount of praise they heaped on the company was embarrassing (well almost). They love our product and the company. They raved about product performance, reliability, competitiveness and more importantly, they were extremely complimentary about the people in the company.

As you know, I have always believed that if you have the best people, you will have an outstandingly successful company. We are blessed with both – outstanding people and an incredible product line. Speaking of product line, the NetScreen-1000 is only just beginning to set the world on fire. Just goes to show you that VCs aren't necessarily the smartest people on the planet!

But, where do we go next? We are about to embark upon another great adventure. Taking the company public will be another great milestone, but it should be viewed as the start of a new chapter in NetScreen's history not the end of the book. We have world-leading products now, but we need to keep ahead of the curve and we need to continue to innovate and be first to market with an expanded product and technology offering. As we move further up the food chain and expand our presence from the enterprise to more core networking customers, we will need to … can develop internally. Going public will give us the currency and opportunity to do just that.

On our fifth birthday, we will be a well established player in the enterprise market (some of the companies that our channel partners are talking to today would astound you), we will own the high performance Internet Data Centre (and US Data Centers), Service Provider, MAN and BLEC space and we will still have technology that is well ahead of the competition. It won't necessarily be an easy ride. I can promise you, though, that it will be an interesting and exciting two years. If we continue to stick to our original principles of hiring the very best, putting customers first, moving fast and eliminating unnecessary overhead and bureaucracy, we will continue to be a company whose people and products receive praise not only from our customers, but also from our harshest critics – ourselves. It won't be easy to achieve these things as we grow and add more great people to our team, but it will be key to our success.

Congratulations on three fantastic years (or part thereof), and let's do it bigger and better in the next …

Robert Thomas has provided his perspective for the inaugural edition of ScreenStories.

new net news

The month of October saw several important NetScreen events. The 2001 Sales Kickoff in Monterey, the Quarterly All-Hands meeting at Techmart in Santa Clara, and the 2000 NetScreen Open/Channel Meeting.

Those of you on email, no doubt saw either this author's summary of the 2001 Sales Kickoff, or Mark Smith's more prosaic evaluation. We won't bore you, our friendly NetScreen readers, with these details again (if you do want the full text just shoot me an email). We thought we'd use this space to focus on a few highlights.

Some of you may not have seen the final results of the "Who Wants to be an Acronymillionaire" contest. For the record, Paul Stach was the big winner of dinner for two (send the bill to Sales!), correctly providing the …

(NetScreen月刊创刊。Robert Thomas的致词)

SCREENSTORIES

Final Edition

April 2004, Volume 28

The Last Chapter – or is it?

Robert Thomas

Robert Thomas from the inaugural Edition of ScreenStories, Nov. 2000

Where do I begin? First things first – I would like to thank you for making NetScreen the incredible success that we are today. I would like to thank you for making NetScreen an amazing place to work and for giving me the most enjoyable working experience that I have ever had.

In the last seven years there has been no other company in Silicon Valley that can match your achievements. The team that we have built at NetScreen is world class and is the reason for our success. It always sounds a little trite when we say that no matter how true it is. However I have never worked with a better, more professional, more dedicated group of people. A great company is built because of the passion and beliefs of the people who are the company. At NetScreen we always seemed to share the same passion and set of beliefs, and we all believed that the impossible could be done – and then we went out and did it!

NetScreen has been in existence for almost seven years. It seems like a long time and a short time. So much has happened that one would have to think we have been in business forever. We have gone from a company with two basic products to a product line that now has hundreds of elements. We have gone from no market share to a leader in our space in every market in the world. We have gone from an unknown company to a well known, well respected one. We have gone public, generated hundreds of millions of dollars in available cash and we have bought and successfully integrated other great companies. We have won countless awards for our technology and we have grown our business every quarter of our life!

And so, what next, how do we keep the success going and go on to even greater heights, perhaps even accelerating our rate of growth? We are lucky at NetScreen – we have choices. We could have chosen to grow organically, acquire the technologies we didn't have and continue the march and the campaign against our competitors. Or we could combine with another larger company with similar views and aspirations to ours. As often happens, the right decision seems to evolve naturally without any con-

the future, a common culture, share the same strategy towards competitive attack (even sharing the same competitor) and are successful in the market place. The NetScreen Juniper pairing is just such a match.

NetScreen is a company about beginnings not endings. We have successfully re-invented ourselves a number of times over the last seven years. We saw our IPO as the beginning of a new phase of our life not the culmination of our efforts. We passed one competitor and rather than rest on our laurels, we set out after the next larger one. The merger with Juniper is another beginning for us and it helps us become the number one network security company in the world, faster and with greater breadth and depth. All of your achievements have made me extremely proud of the NetScreen team and I know, as we become Juniper, you will continue to make me proud of your efforts. We will find a good home at Juniper for our passion and our belief that we can do anything. We will go on to even bigger successes as a combined company. This is definitely not the last chapter – we haven't even begun yet!

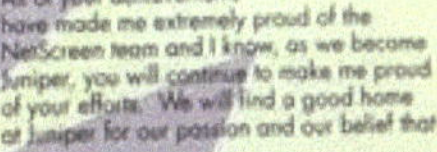

NetScreen office locations throughout the years.

1.	355 W. Olive Avenue, Suite 101	Sunnyvale
2.	4699 Old Ironsides Road	Sunnyvale
3.	2860 San Tomas Expressway	Sunnyvale
4.	350 Oakmead Parkway	Sunnyvale
5.	805 11th Ave, Bldg 3, Ariba Campus	Sunnyvale

(NetScreen月刊最后一期，Robert Thomas的致词)

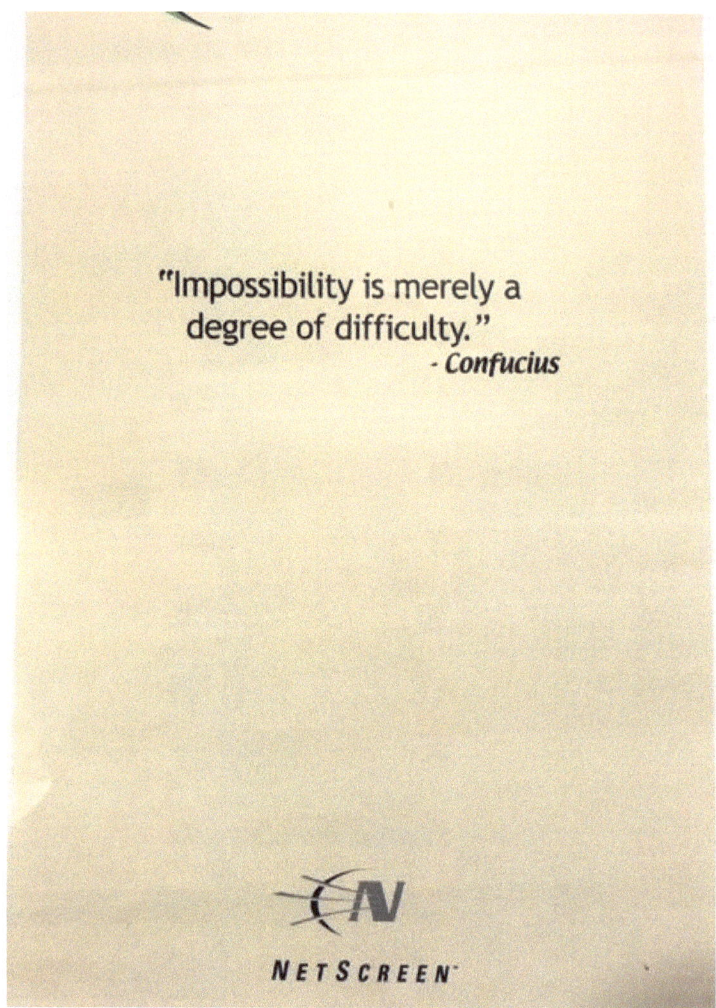
"Impossibility is merely a
degree of difficulty."
- Confucius
NETSCREEN

SCREENSTORIES

February 2001, Volume 3

Feng [illegible] and Yan [illegible] Core of a Great [illegible]

T[illegible] on where the company [illegible] says a lot, then, [illegible] first thing they said [illegible] go on the front page [illegible] be tucked inside.

"It is the individual [illegible] tant," said Feng. "Your day [illegible] work is as important as ours to the company's success, that's the message I want to get to all employees." Yan continued Feng's point. "We are grateful that we have the greatest team, they are motivated, talented and disciplined. To win you have to have a good team and we have been able to bring in the best."

Feng and Yan would know about building a great team, they've been building one at NetScreen for more than three years. When they first got started, though, things weren't quite so clear. "There wasn't one specific day when we woke up with an idea to found an Internet security company," said Feng. "We just felt that we wanted to do something on our own."

One thing was clear, Feng and Yan knew they could trust each other, after all, they'd known each other since 1981 when they met on their first day at Tinghua University in Beijing. "Actually, Yan was late. He came up, staring at me and asked if he was in the right place," said Feng. "It was only orientation," explained Yan. "It wasn't like I was late for class."

Feng and Yan were close from that day on, they were roommates, and kept in touch after they graduated. Yan came to the U.S. before Feng and got his Ph.D. in computer science from Johns Hopkins University. After a stint as an assistant professor at the University of Saskatchewan, Yan moved to the Silicon Valley where he got a job with Cisco. Feng decided to come to the states after the 1989 Tiananmen Square Event. Two years later, he also moved to the Valley and took a job with Intel. It didn't take long for them to start talking about founding their own company.

"At the time, this was around 1997, I had been in the Valley for five or six years," said Yan. "I'd seen a lot of people leave big companies and start new businesses, so I knew it was achievable."

But in the beginning, talking was all they were doing. "We had a vague idea," said Feng, "so we started meeting once a week in my living room. Then it became twice a week, and eventually we were meeting every day." There was also a third founder, Ken Xie, who had been working at Healtheon (later WebMD). Between the three of them they had all the elements that would provide the core of NetScreen: Ken at Healtheon knew the importance of securing confidential patient data; Feng at Intel had the chip and system design experience; and Yan with Cisco had the software and networking experience.

"For the first few months there was not a lot of engineering," said Feng, "we mostly talked about marketing and ideas. Once we targeted Internet security, there were three main points we focused on, and they are still true today. First, was network performance. At the time network performance was typically 100Mbps, with a software firewall that speed dropped to 10Mbps. It was clear that this wouldn't do. If you look now, the differential is about the same. Network traffic rates continue to grow, so security must grow with it. Second, was integration of firewalls with VPN equipment. There was a demand for firewalls, but VPNs hadn't taken off. Basically, they are the same devices, both firewalls and VPNs screen the network packets, but no one had put them together in one device. Third, was total ease of management. We saw how difficult people were finding it to deploy a firewall, and we wanted to simplify the configuration and installation process. We were one of the first companies to have a Web-based GUI, and our transparent mode firewall meant customers wouldn't have to reconfigure the network to install it. These are still key principles that drive engineering every day: performance, integration and simplicity."

"The company is now becoming more mature," said Yan. "If you look at the different stages of a company, there's a technology stage, a product stage and a management stage. We've entered that management stage. It's critical now that all parts of the team meet their objectives." "Many people ask me what I think the most important thing is to make a company successful," Feng continues. "My answer would be: it's neither a smart idea, nor a killer product. The two most important things are a great team and flawless execution."

new net news

It was a landmark month for NetScreen, one in which we moved to new offices and celebrated our most successful quarter to date. We also announced our managing director in Latin America, many of you had already met Francisco Arguedas (aka Packo), but we made it official with a press release. Additionally, we went to the COMNET Conference &

NetScreen Expands Operations in Latin America to Serve Growing Internet Security Market

Company Announces Managing Director and Two New Distributors in the Region

Santa Clara, CA (Jan. 17, 2001): NetScreen Technologies, a leading developer of ASIC-based Internet security systems and appliances, today announced the appointment of Francisco Arguedas as managing director, Latin America. Arguedas is responsible for overseeing all aspects of marketing and sales

Arguedas has been instrumental in signing two new NetScreen distributors in Latin America. ICON Sistemas Informaticos is now an authorized NetScreen distributor for the Mercosur region covering Argentina, Uruguay, Paraguay, Chile and Peru. ESoluciones has been named an authorized distributor in the Andean Pact countries, including: Columbia, Venezu-

Barbara at a glance Barbara at a glance

NetScreen-5200 and NetScreen-208 Score Awards

NetScreen stole the show at the recent Networks Telecom Show in the UK. The NetScreen-5200 took top honors as Best of Show—the most important of all new products introduced there, while the NetScreen-208 won Best Security Product of the Year. Any company would be ecstatic to win one award, but to win both, as Mark Smith would say, is *UNBELIEVABLE*.

NetScreen Co-Founders Named Entrepreneurs of the Year

Our own Feng Deng and Yan Ke took the spotlight on Friday, June 21, at the Fairmont Hotel in San Jose as they were presented the Northern California Entrepreneur of the Year Award for Technology. The event, sponsored by Ernst & Young, was the culmination of a selection process that received hundreds of nominations from Northern California companies

Continued on page 2

New Net News

S-1 Party

The last two months have set new standards for craziness at NetScreen – milestones have been reached such as the company's four-year anniversary, significant events in NetScreen's evolution such as the filing of our S-1 registration statement, and many new products and product features have been introduced – all in an altered economic and political climate that renders incalculable stress on everyone.

Everyone at NetScreen should take tremendous pride with the position we are in: a great company with a great product at the right time.

From a financial and legal perspective, I have never seen a financial organization collectively and unconditionally come together and basically put their lives on hold to accomplish something as significant as the S-1. The legal department just amazes me; Tom Kovar led the charge on the S-1, but his group was behind him assisting on the S-1 and making sure from a legal perspective NetScreen was timely and professionally serviced.

Completing the S-1 and being a public company opens up many opportunities for NetScreen to continue to grow and be the leader in the Internet security sector. It is the beginning of a new, exciting and challenging chapter in our development.

Everyone involved in the S-1 process did an outstanding job, one person stands out, though and that was Tom Kovar. Tom was in his environment and truly did an exceptional job. Tom was the person who pushed the button filing the S-1, and that is a great honor."

I think everyone will agree that Rosun, as well, has been an invaluable addition to the NetScreen team, like a late-season addition to a ballclub who provides that added spark to push the team into the playoffs.

And, that late-season drive has included many other events that we will mention briefly below. We think everyone will agree it has been a frenzied and exciting two months for NetScreen.

September 19

NetScreen Introduces Additional High Availability Features to Secure Mission Critical Networks

October 2

NetScreen Simplifies Deployment, Extends the Reach and Improves Management of VPNs with Latest Version of ScreenOS

October 22

NetScreen Launches Global Alliance Program to Deliver Customer-Focused Network Security Sol…

Through the new Global Alliance Program, NetScreen will … leading companies to deliver customer-focused solutions … the scope of network security within enterprise and carrier infrastructures and managed services. At the launch of the … 12 alliance members are working with NetScreen to deliver … solutions to customers: dynamicsoft, Ericsson, Extreme …, Foundry Networks, Internet Security Solutions, Inc., … NetIQ, Radware, Resonate Technologies™, … Trend Micro, and Websense.

NetScreen Announces Intrusion Detection and … Support as Part of its Global Alliance Program

NetScreen announced a new program and new product… will improve the means by which enterprises and carri… mission-critical content on their networks.

NetScreen Acquires OneSecure

As all of you know by now, NetScreen signed an agreement in August to acquire OneSecure, Inc., and completed the acquisition September 19, 2002.

DEPARTMENT: R & D

Bryan Burns

Arnit Green

Kowsik Guruswamy
Manager, Software Engineering

Siu-Wang Leung
Staff Software Engineer

Jens Schmidt
Manager, Software Engineering

Aaron Turner
Senior Security Engineer

Song Wang
Senior Software Engineer

Kent Watsen
Software Architect

Alan Greenfield
Senior Software Engineer

Chris Husing
Technical Writer III

Chris Iezzoni
Test Engineer

Joy Ying Jiang
Senior Test Engineer

Usamah Asim Malik
Software Engineer

John Metzler
Senior Software Engineer

Heidi Miller
Technical Writer I

Eric Moret
Senior Security Engineer

Ronit Polak
Staff Test Engineer

Radhika Rayadu Vooruvakili
Software Engineer

Ivetta Starikova
Software Engineer

Aileen Young
Test Engineer

James Fehrle
Senior Software Engineer

DEPARTMENT: Sales

Chris Cantrell
Manager, Systems Engineering

Roger Hegland
Vice President, Sales

Mark Alfieri
Enterprise Account Executive

Daniel Burns
Director, Enterprise Western Region

Monte Sjobakken
Director, Channel Sales (Central Region)

Stuart Hoffmann
Sr. Systems Engineer

Wayne Maw
Channel Account Executive

Mechelle Moore
Channel Account Executive

Jim Pickering
Enterprise Account Executive

Steve Richards
Sr. Systems Engineer

Takeshi Suganuma
Consulting Systems Engineer

Jim Pickering
Enterprise Account Executive

DEPARTMENT: Marketing

Heidi Fisher
Product Manager

Ajit Sanchetti
Senior Product Manager

Sarah Sorenson
Product Marketing Manager

Benedict Kee

DEPARTMENT: IT

Moshe Shaham

Wendy Wilser
Program Manager

DEPARTMENT: Customer Service

Lisa Kapul

Anthony Lauria

Teodorie Ravara

Avishai Avivi

For more detailed information about the OneSecure acquisition, you can access a number of documents on our Web site http://www.netscreen.com

A Year After the IPO by Robert Thomas

Last month, we celebrated our first birthday as a public company. I think this is an excellent time to stop and reflect on going public, consider what we accomplished over the past year, and to also look forward to see where we are going.

December 2001 was [illegible] time around NetScreen, but to [illegible] the challenges of going public [illegible] to consider what was going on [illegible] markets around that time. The technology [illegible] had already started. Telcos and [illegible] were losing money [illegible]. A lot of the small players in the technology [illegible], especially startup companies, were having trouble getting funding. In all of 2001 there were only five or six technology companies that succeeded in going public. All the investment banks were setting the bar very high because the market was collapsing and technology itself was no longer perceived as a good investment.

At the time, NetScreen had roughly $30 million in cash. We were getting close to being cash flow positive. We didn't really need to do a public offering to raise money to survive. From a cash point of view, we could just continue doing what we were doing. Frankly, we thought going to the public market for money was a little risky. So why DID we decide to do it?

As we began selling to larger companies, particularly the financial services firms like Schwab, Fidelity, and UBS Paine Webber, we'd win the deal after a three or four month sales campaign. But then we would spend just as much time convincing them that we were viable and would still be here tomorrow. As a public company, we believed we wouldn't have to face that added level of due diligence and delay. **We needed the credibility as a public company to sell to the Fortune 500.**

We hoped that investors would understand our story and recognize the strength of our numbers, giving us a successful IPO. Our concerns were soon [illegible]. We put 10 million shares on the market and we got orders from institutional investors for 270 million shares—a 27-fold oversubscription!

I think **there were two reasons for this success.** First, we had a very strong story to tell financially, and the networking security market was very hot—and still is. Second, there was such a lack of opportunity to invest in technology because so few companies could make it over the hurdles set by bankers.

On December 12, the day NetScreen went public, we were standing on the trading floor in New York. It was one of those once-in-a-lifetime experiences, seeing NetScreen's ticker symbol appear for the first time and then appearing again and again as the stock traded. It's something I will never forget. We enjoyed the experience. A day later it was business as usual.

There was also a lot of pressure on us now and we were concerned about disappointing the financial community. The first year of life as a public company is always a tenuous one. A new public company is under the microscope. One small slip can be devastating. Combine that with an economic environment in which the economy is terrible, IT spending is depressed, and companies are collapsing, and you have many pitfalls that we could fall into our first year. It could have affected our credibility, our stock price, and even our viability.

We saw the IPO as a great step forward for the company—but just a step. We needed to continue to focus on doing great things and improving the company and the product and getting more customers. On the financial side, we made sure that the year was as well planned as it could be and that we didn't make any promises to the financial community that we didn't have a 90 or 95 percent probability of meeting. And we focused on things like reducing cost throughout the year to make sure we didn't get giddy with the $150 million we had in the bank.

Looking back over our first year as a public company, our concerns were unfounded, and what we did achieve was amazing. We've almost completely turned over our product line, introducing many, many new products. We introduced a brand new ASIC, our third-generation silicon was completed and went into products.

We were profitable in our first quarter as a public company and profitable every quarter of the year. We grew by at least double digits every quarter. Our profitability has improved every quarter during the year, generating about $43 million in positive cash. Our market share increased every quarter, and every quarter of the year we took market share from our competitors.

We acquired our first company. The integration of that company has been about as seamless as we could have hoped. Acquiring a company is always a risky thing, but the people in OneSecure fit our culture perfectly. The technology is complimentary to ours and we're integrating it much more easily than we expected.

We've retained all the people, and they are very enthusiastic, which is a great asset. You string all those successes together, and I think there is nothing that can compare to the year that we've had at NetScreen.

Of course, the reason for our success is people. We didn't experience what some companies do, this 180-degree turn from dedication and hard work to sitting back and thinking about the stock price. We are blessed with a group of people who think more long term than today's stock price. I think we have a very unselfish team spirit and family oriented attitude at NetScreen. Everyone knows we are in it together, and what each of us does everyday helps the other 499 people at NetScreen. They feel part of something bigger than themselves.

I would say NetScreen people are extremely loyal and hard working. There is great pride in being a NetScreen employee. We enjoy what we do. That's a great testament to the kind of people that are hired and the kind of attitude they have. It's all about a winning mentality.

Given this attitude and success, I believe we can go on to bigger and better things in the future. **Our survival depends, to a large degree, on growth.** Last year, we had revenues of about $140 million. This year we will be considerably above $200 million. We need to get to a billion dollars sometime in the next four years or so, just to maintain viability as a company.

We can't do that by doing what we do today, selling the same kind of products to the same people. We have to [illegible] leaps. We have to [illegible] might be different ways of selling our product, or different technologies that we acquire or develop to make it a product that appeals to a broader set of customers. There are a lot of things that we need to do to change the scale of our business to get to this billion-dollar number.

We will continue to do innovative things in the networking and security space that continually broaden our offerings, giving us more complete customer solutions. We will accomplish this through a lot of different efforts: more development, acquisitions, and licensing of technology.

If we are going to do all that over the next few years, it means the same kind of dedication, commitment, enthusiasm, and hard work that we've seen over the last four years. We have a great shot at that. With our can-do attitude, if our objective is to be a billion-dollar company in the next four years, we will get there.

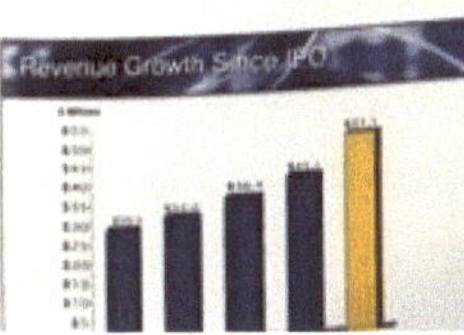

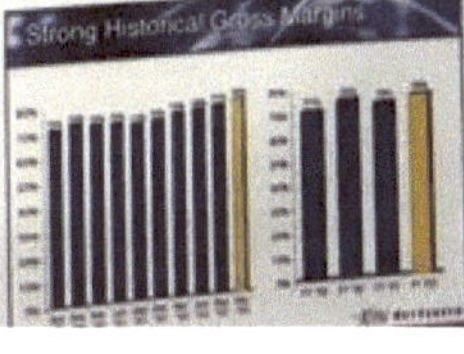

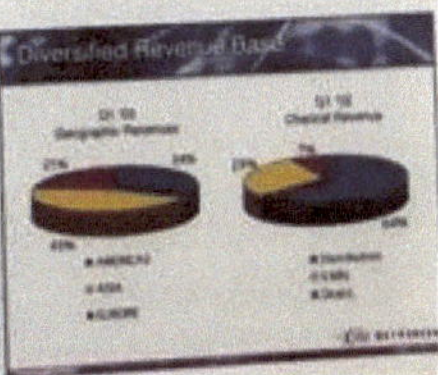

that you live by that you would like to share with your fellow NetScreen'ers?

"Be excellent to each other"

ıgazine about sponsor-
stically speaking
mainstream publication
reat publicity. The story
tive noir style by a net-
at a large bank helped
here an employee was
ıs and siphoning off
e photos would show
competition's box as a

ou think are the
reen, what kind of
nk it is, what kind
want it to be?

es of NetScreen are
er satisfaction in our
port, and to outsmart the
implement features and

be is a company that
and to build cutting edge
esses communication
hat comes with growth by
ts business processes while
customer satisfaction.

f Virgin Corporation, said
Radio that, "the employee
customer, and in doing
inspiring the employee,
hich equals happy share-
ning Herb Kelleher, head
lieves in as well. So it's my
nt to keep us inspired and
e need to take care of our
a challenge to those not in
ellent to each other" (in the
ilosophers Bill and Ted).

NEOTERIS

NetScreen To Acquire Neoteris

As all of you know by now, NetScreen signed an agreement to acquire Neoteris, Inc.

Founded in May of 2000, Neoteris, Inc. is the market leader in the SSL VPN product category as well as a leader in the application security gateway market, with more than 550 enterprise customers and approximately one million users worldwide.

The acquisition will expand NetScreen's product portfolio to include Neoteris' market leading "clientless" SSL remote access VPN solution that enables an enterprise remote user, telecommuter, or extranet partner to easily and securely access corporate resources via a standard web browser. NetScreen will also leverage Neoteris' technology and expertise to accelerate the integration of application-level security into the network infrastructure.

For more detailed information about the Neoteris, Inc. acquisition, you can access documents on our web site http://

NetScreen's Memory Lane
PEPSI

Halloween Howls

NetScreen Co-Founders Named
Entrepreneurs of the Year
Northern California Entrepreneurs Award for Technology

DRIVEN
All Hands Worldwide Meeting
October 4, 2003

1997 - 2001
ANNIVERSARY
4 Years and Counting

Changming Liu
What changes have you seen since you've been here?
CL: Employee enthusiasm. Keep motivating and empowering its employees. People are one of the most important assets of any successful company.

Brian Kerr
What's the best NetScreen freebie you've received?
BK: If you're trying to catch me for stealing NetScreen stuff from the company, I plead guilty. I have one beta unit from the first batch of NetScreen-100s that's sitting in my cube - just a classic. That and I have a NetScreen-5 that I use at home.

David Tran
What core corporate characteristic of NetScreen would you most like to see survive?
DT: Teamwork spirit where everyone at NetScreen is really a team player and is willing to go the extra mile. No matter how large we will be later, the combination of a powerful team spirit and a willingness to go the extra mile will help all of us to overcome any number of obstacles that can get in our way of more success.

Exerpts from 4 Years and Counting, ScreenStories, Oct/Nov. 2001, Vol.11

2003
Worldwide Corporate
Kickoff Meeting

NetScreen Acquires...

OneSecure

NetScreen will make OneSecure Intrusion Detection and Prevention (IDP) solution immediately available as the NetScreen IDP-100 appliance in the U.S., Canada and selected countries within Europe and Asia. This allows us to enter the potentially very large intrusion detection system (IDS) market, estimated at over $1 billion within the next three years-too big for us to ignore.

NEOTERIS

NetScreen to Acquire Neoteris
The acquisition will expand NetScreen's product portfolio to include Neoteris' market leading "clientless" SSL remote access VPN solution that enables an enterprise remote user, telecommuter, or extranet partner to easily and securely access corporate resources via a standard web browser. NetScreen will also leverage Neoteris' technology and expertise to accelerate the integration of application-level security into the network infrastructure.

A Year After the IPO

We needed the credibility as a public company to sell to the Fortune 500.

There was also a lot of pressure on us now and we were concerned about disappointing the financial community.

Of course, the reason for our success is people.

Exerpts from A Year After the IPO, Robert Thomas, Screen Stories, Feb/Mar. 2003, Vol.20

Looking back over our first year as a public company, our concerns were unfounded, and what we did achieve was amazing.

Our survival depends, to a large degree, on growth.

We will continue to do innovative things in the networking and security space that continually broaden our offerings, giving us more complete customer solutions.

Truly Amazing! You're Awesome! Wow! Good Going!

Congratulations to the APAC Sales Team!
APAC Revenue for Q1 2003
Surpassed Check Point!

This is Incredible! Stupendous! This is Success!

NetScreen Confidential - for internal employee use only

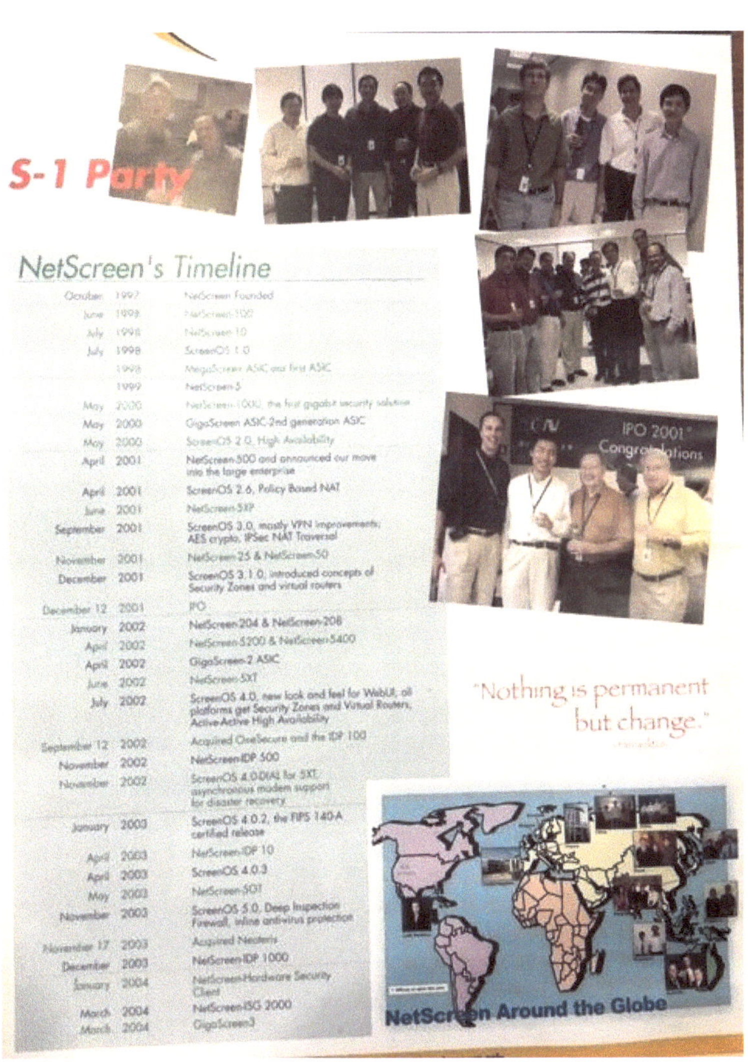

NetScreen's Timeline

October	1997	NetScreen Founded
June	1998	NetScreen-100
July	1998	NetScreen-10
July	1998	ScreenOS 1.0
	1998	MegaScreen ASIC our first ASIC
	1999	NetScreen-5
May	2000	NetScreen-1000, the first gigabit security solution
May	2000	GigaScreen ASIC-2nd generation ASIC
May	2000	ScreenOS 2.0, High Availability
April	2001	NetScreen-500 and announced our move into the large enterprise
April	2001	ScreenOS 2.6, Policy Based NAT
June	2001	NetScreen-5XP
September	2001	ScreenOS 3.0, mostly VPN improvements; AES crypto, IPSec NAT Traversal
November	2001	NetScreen-25 & NetScreen-50
December	2001	ScreenOS 3.1.0, introduced concepts of Security Zones and virtual routers
December 12	2001	IPO
January	2002	NetScreen-204 & NetScreen-208
April	2002	NetScreen-5200 & NetScreen-5400
April	2002	GigaScreen-2 ASIC
June	2002	NetScreen-5XT
July	2002	ScreenOS 4.0, new look and feel for WebUI, all platforms get Security Zones and Virtual Routers, Active-Active High Availability
September 12	2002	Acquired OneSecure and the IDP 100
November	2002	NetScreen-IDP 500
November	2002	ScreenOS 4.0.0DIAL for 5XT, asynchronous modem support for disaster recovery
January	2003	ScreenOS 4.0.2, the FIPS 140-A certified release
April	2003	NetScreen-IDP 10
April	2003	ScreenOS 4.0.3
May	2003	NetScreen-5GT
November	2003	ScreenOS 5.0, Deep Inspection Firewall, inline antivirus protection
November 17	2003	Acquired Neoteris
December	2003	NetScreen-IDP 1000
January	2004	NetScreen-Hardware Security Client
March	2004	NetScreen-ISG 2000
March	2004	GigaScreen3

Wanted by NetScreen

NSCN

附录四，硅谷大陆创业上市公司略考

硅谷来自大陆的华人的创业基本上可以分为2次比较大的浪潮。第一次是1994年到1998年左右；第二次是1999年到2001年左右。第三次浪潮从2005年到现在，大陆工程师创业呈现爆发性的成长，大多数都还在创业阶段的各个阶段。本文的调查范围局限在曾经在美国NYSE或者NASDAQ上公开发行股票（IPO）的公司。时间范围在1990-2010年期间。

另外，在创办人方面，我们局限在在大陆完成了其本科教育的，后来来美国留学或者研发的工程师，科学家。

× 大陆华人第一次创业浪潮（1994-1998）

典型代表公司：

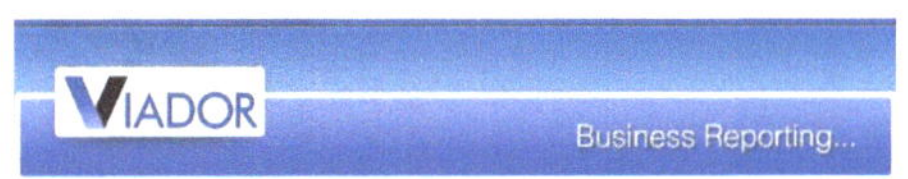

Viador

创办人： WANG Xi

创办时间： 1994年

业务: 提供公司ecommerce软件和服务。

上市日期：1999年10月26日

目前状况：

在2000年的dot com的股灾中,受到严重影响，成为低于1美金的股票。2001年7月，Viador被NASDAQ通知股票被停盘交易。

Viador是改革开放以来第一家由大陆留学生创办的上市公司。

GRIC (GOREMOTE INTERNET COMMUNICATIONS)
创办人：CHEN Hong
创办时间：1994年
业务:提供全球的网络IP电话服务
上市日期：1999年12月15日
目前状况：
2005年12月12日，iPass（IPAS）以7千6百50万美金的现金收购GRIC公司。截至2016年10月，iPass目前市值约为1亿美金，股价为1美金左右。

Omnivision
创办人： Chen Datong, He XinPing etc
创办时间：1995年
业务: 数字图像传感器， 摄像头芯片设计和生产公司
上市日期：2000年7月14日
目前状况：2016年1月28日， Omni Vision与由北京清芯华创投资管理有限公司、中信资本控股有限公司和金石投资有限公司组成的财团（“中国财团”）联合宣布，中国财团已完成对Omni Vision的私有化收购，交易总金额约19亿美元。

WebEx
创办人： Min Zhu
创办时间： 1995年2月
业务: 提供基于IP的远程网络视频会议系统。
上市日期：2000年7月31日
目前状况：
2007年3月15日，思科以29亿美金的价格收购WebEx。

Avanex
创办人：Xiaofan Cao等
创办时间：1997年
业务：高密度波长多任务器
上市日期： 2000年2月。NASDAQ代号：AVNX
目前状态：2009年4月，Avanex与Bookham合并成一个新公司Oclaro。合并之后Avanex部分占到合并后新公司总股份的46.75%

NETSCREEN

Netscreen

创办人： Deng Feng, Ke Yan and Qin Xie

创办时间：1998年10月
业务: 基于硬件和芯片加速的高性能防火墙，IDS，VPN系统
上市日期：2001年12月。NASDAQ代号为NSCN
目前状况：
2004年4月，Juniper Networks以41亿美金的价格收购NetScreen。

第一波华人创业公司特点：

退出周期：从创办到上市，平均时间是4到5年。
目前状况：全部退市或者已经被收购

× 大陆华人第二次创业浪潮（1999-2001）
典型代表公司：

Telenav
创办人：Haiping Jin
创办时间：1999年
业务：提供个人和商业的地理信息GPS服务
上市时间：2010年5月在NASDAQ上市，代号为TNAV
目前状况：市值为2.5亿美金。2016年财务年的总收入为1.83亿美金。其中，来自车载GPS服务的收入1.35亿

美金，占总收入的74%。

Fortinet
创办人： Ken Xie等
创办时间： 2000年11月
业务：提供UTM，NGFW等高端网络安全设备
上市时间：2009年11月18日。NASDAQ代号为FTNT。
目前状况：
Fortinet目前市值为59亿美金。2015年的总营业额为10亿美金左右。

Spreadtrum
创办人： Ping Wu等
创办时间： 2001年
业务：无线GSM，TD-CDMA芯片
上市时间：2007年7月。NASDAQ：SPRD
目前状况：2013年12月，紫光集团通过18亿美金现金的方式私募化展讯科技。展讯从美国NASDAQ退市。

Datadomain

创办人： Kai Li等

创办时间： 2001年

业务：Data Storage Backup System

上市时间：2007年6月27日。NASDAQ：DUUP

目前状况：2009年6月，EMC以24亿美金的价格收购。

第二波华人创业公司特点：

退出周期： 从创办到上市，平均时间是5-10年。

目前状况：部分选择了战略性退市，目标回到中国A股，或者还在美股市场上。

www.ingramcontent.com/pod-product-compliance
Lightning Source LLC
LaVergne TN
LVHW012315070326
832902LV00001BA/2

* 9 7 8 1 5 3 9 7 7 4 5 9 4 *